GENERAL PATTON'S PRINCIPLES

★ ★ ★ ★

I remember

GENERAL PATTON'S PRINCIPLES

by

Porter B. Williamson

MSC
Management and Systems Consultants, Inc.
Tucson, Arizona 85717

PATTON'S PRINCIPLES

Other books by the author:
ARIZONA REAL ESTATE LAWS
ARIZONA PROPERTY TAX LAWS
ARIZONA ZONING AND SUBDIV. LAWS
STRENGTH FROM WEAKNESS

Editorial columns by the author:
THESE RIGHTS ARE YOURS
SELLING TO THE GOVERNMENT

Copyright — 1979 Porter B. Williamson
Copyright under the Berne Convention

Library of Congress Catalog Number — 77-70779
ISBN Number — 0-918356-03-2

First Printing

Publisher
Management and Systems Consultants, Inc.
University Station, #40457
Tucson, Arizona 85717
United States of America

CONTENTS

CHAPTER 1
INTRODUCTION

CHAPTER 2
PRINCIPLES OF COMMAND AND MANAGEMENT

"God is truth" is an Old Testament principle which Gen. Patton followed. He spoke the truth when it was unpopular to speak truth. By his words and his actions he constantly attempted to get at the basic truth of every situation. He slapped the man who needed to be slapped. Ten years after the face slapping incident, this man admitted Gen. Patton had every right to give more severe discipline than a slap. This man admitted, in a newspaper interview, "Maybe if I had played it right I could have gotten home a lot sooner."

This basic Patton Principle, God is truth, is not discussed in this book because every Patton Principle is basic truth. To report the truth about Gen. Patton is more difficult than trying to report the many legends. The problem is the truth is more unusual than the legend. I entitled this book, **I Remember Gen. Patton's Principles**, because I can write only of what I can document and remember.

Many readers who served with Gen. Patton will know that I have not listed all of his principles. Not all of his expressions resulted in some event which could be reported. It would be difficult to give examples for the following principles: "Every man is expendable, including generals, if the results warrant it." Other principles which would be difficult to connect with an event would be, "If we run out of food, we will eat the enemy or each other!" and "A pint of sweat will save a gallon of blood."

I regret that I cannot remember all of the phrases used by Gen. Patton. He was the king of all phrase makers. His barbs of truth sharpened the minds of every listener.

I have tried to imitate Gen. Patton's talent for using machine gun bursts of words. Between the short bursts of words, he would pause to let the troops enjoy a laugh or to absorb the full truth of his statement. Gen. Patton held the attention of every man when he spoke, and he said as much with his carefully timed silent periods as he did with his short sentences. Many readers will puzzle over the absence of profanity. No one could imitate Gen. Patton's profanity.

PREFACE

After reading every book about Gen. Patton, it was my personal opinion that the writers missed the true personality of Gen. Patton. For example, several writers called him arrogant, flamboyant, and foolhardy. No writer caught the truth that great leaders must act arrogant and flamboyant. No writer caught the importance of the pistols, the arrogant lectures, and the flamboyant actions as the carefully rehearsed and planned actions of a man who knew how to act to lead men into combat with the enemy and with death. No writer who called Gen. Patton foolhardy caught the importance of immediate pursuit of the retreating enemy. No writer caught the humility and the religion of Gen. Patton. I have written of Gen. Patton as I remember him.

I will always treasure the words of his son who commented on the manuscript saying, "I know my dad would be proud to ha e his principles sorted out by you."

Porter B. Williamson

CHAPTER I

INTRODUCTION

WE CAN ALWAYS LEARN FROM EACH OTHER

I served with General George S. Patton Jr. No man served **under** Gen. Patton; he was always serving **with** us. In truth, I still serve with Gen. Patton, and he continues to serve with me. He makes me take cold showers, he makes me take deep breaths, and he makes me pull in my bushel of blubber.

He served with me when the doctors told me I had terminal cancer. He told me, "Did you ever stop to think that death could be more exciting than life?"

When I fall he tells me, "The test of success is not what you do when you are on top. Success is how high you bounce when you hit bottom."

When I have a difficult decision to make, he tells me, "No decision is difficult to make if you get all of the facts."

When I get alarmed, he says, "Never take counsel of your fears."

When my fears get too high, he scolds, "Fear kills more people than death."

When I get angry and want to strike back in revenge, he orders, "Don't forget revenge belongs to God."

I will relate Gen. Patton's principles as I remember them and try to separate the facts from the many legends. Facts and legends about Gen. Patton are difficult to separate because so many legends were told about Gen. Patton during his life. An additional problem is that many of the legends about Gen. Patton are not as amazing as his actual achievements. Gen. Patton was a genius if a genius is a man with ideas thirty years ahead of the leaders of society. Gen. Patton combined the genius of a military leader with the talents of a religious scholar.

My first meeting with Gen. Patton was on a bridge over a small stream in South Carolina. It was a chilly afternoon in November, 1941, a few days before Pearl Harbor. We were on maneuvers (war games) with the I Armored Corps. In a few months the I Armored Corps would have over fifty thousand men. In November, 1941, the I Armored

Corps had a dozen officers and less than a hundred men. The I Armored Corps had been authorized ("created") in the mid-year of 1941. In the few months since authorization, only a limited amount of arms and equipment had been received. We did have an abundance of staff cars because staff cars were exactly the same as the civilian cars except for the G.I. drab color.

Early in the maneuvers, our I Armored Corps received the orders that Gen. Patton's 2nd Armored Division would be under our command for the Carolina maneuvers. Gen. Patton's reputation was so well known that our G-4 Supply Officer asked for a transfer. This Regular Army Colonel was a competent and well trained officer. When he learned that he had to supply gasoline and rations to Gen. Patton's Division, the Colonel said, "There is no possible way supplies can be delivered to that 'Hell on Wheels' Division. We do not have the trucks nor the cans nor the men! I am getting out of I Armored Corps. I am not going to be made to look like a fool at this stage of my military career."

"Hell on Wheels" was the name   Gen. Patton had given to his Division to indicate the speed they would travel. "Cans" were the usual five gallon gas cans now available in war surplus stores. Refueling an armored tank in the field required that the gasoline in five gallon cans   be carried by the men. Gasoline tank trucks could not roll through the fields nor could the tank trucks be exposed to aircraft attacks. The gasoline was pumped (milked) into the five gallon cans and might be carried by the men for many hundred yards. The large trucks could not go through the mud and fields as easily as the track laying tanks.

With our Corps G-4 Officer transferred, the task of keeping Gen. Patton supplied with gasoline fell upon me, the only other G-4 Officer on the I Armored Corps Staff. As a first lieutenant, I could fail as I was advised by our

Chief of Staff. The failure would be based on my lack of military experience since I was a civilian reserve officer. Despite the lack of experience, I was determined to do the best I could whether I failed or not. I did not intend to make a career in the military.

As I review the events now, thirty-five years later, I am certain that this Carolina war game was a maneuver to cause Gen. Patton to be ineffective with the new things called "tanks." The old line officers in the infantry, field artillery and cavalry wanted to win all wars. The new tanks changed all of the ideas about how to win wars. The horse cavalry existed in name without any horses, but the old line officers continued to think horse tactics. Gen. Patton was the Billy Mitchell of the new armored tanks. One way to prove that the tanks would be ineffective in war would be to cut off Gen. Patton's gas supply.

As the Acting G-4 Officer I had my own staff car and driver. This staff car was exactly the same as that given to Generals except I did not have a flag to indicate any rank. First Lieutenants did not have a flag! This car was assigned to me because there was nothing else available.

I had a good relationship with our I Armored Corps Chief of Staff, the first officer in rank under the Commanding General. It was this senior Colonel who advised me that I could fail without causing any loss in efficiency points for my military file. I talked to the Chief of Staff about my authority as the acting G-4 Officer, how much money I could spend, and what procedures to follow. After many years of cutting the money for an adequate defense, Congress in 1941 wanted to get money to the Army as fast as possible. We had more money than we could spend. With the help of the Chief of Staff I secured the proper papers to spend any amount of money that might be necessary to get gasoline to Gen. Patton's 2nd Armored Division. With this authorization, my impressive staff car, and driver, I set out to do the best I could.

All of the gasoline for our use was in railroad tank cars in a city about seventy miles from the combat area. There was ample gasoline, but the gasoline was too far away. We did not have the tank trucks nor any standard GI trucks to haul the five gallon cans. From my inexperienced view, the solution seemed easy — move the gasoline by rail.

With this plan in mind, and a driver, we drove to where our gas was located. I carried all of my papers into the railroad office to talk with the officials. In November of 1941, with the war raging in Europe, civilians would do anything to help with the war games. I asked that the gasoline tank cars be moved to the battle area and "spotted" (parked) on a railroad track which was higher than the land along the side of the tracks. With the tank cars elevated, we could use gravity to fill the little cans and forget about needing any "milkers" to pump the gas into the cans. With luck we might fill the tanks directly from the railroad cars. There was a major problem. It was Saturday! No train crews were on duty to move the tank cars.

As I recall the conversation, I can understand the attitude of the railroad officials. They could not believe that a young first Lieutenant could spend so much money. After a few telephone calls, the officials said it could be done. Many little problems remained as major hurdles: overtime pay, approval from the train dispatchers in charge of the trains already on the tracks, and a secretary to type a large bundle of forms. I could type so I typed the forms for the railroad. While we waited for the train crew, we studied the railroad maps. I drew a circle around the area where we needed the gasoline. There were numerous calls to my boss, the Chief of Staff for the I Armored Corps. I wanted to be sure that moving the gas by rail did not break any of the war game rules. The Chief of Staff confirmed all of our plans.

I did not leave the railroad office until the train crew was moving the tank cars out of the yard. All trains were to take the side-tracks and wait for the tank cars. The railroad officials were kind and did not make an excessive charge for the special train crew. Finally, my driver and I left for the area where the train crew would park the tank cars.

Several hours later I met the train at the elevated track near a highway. We parked the tank cars about two hundred feet apart to make it easier for the armored tanks to pull in for gasoline. There was sufficient gravity for the gasoline to flow into the armored tanks, trucks or cans without the use of any gasoline milking machine. Everything seemed perfect! A row of trees protected the refueling operation from vision. My new problem was how to get the information to Gen. Patton's Headquarters. Nothing would be gained if the 2nd Armored, the Hell on Wheels Division, did not know where the gas was located.

I did not have any success in trying to reach Gen. Patton's Headquarters because they were not connected to any public telephone system. In 1941 we did not have many short wave radios for our military vehicles. I did reach our Corps Headquarters and relayed the location of the gasoline. The instructions to the 2nd Armored Division had to be exact. It would be foolish to send twelve thousand men with tanks and trucks down a rural highway looking for a row of tank cars.

Time was short. At midnight the 2nd Armored Division would be moving. I could see that our plans would be a total failure if the 2nd Armored Division could not get the gasoline. I was beginning to understand the reason the senior colonel wanted to be far away when the war games started. I could see that I could be charged with wasting money to put gasoline in the wrong place.

I directed my driver to use country roads going towards the area where the 2nd Armored Division was reported to be. I wanted to find some troops wearing the colors of the 2nd Armored Division so that I could find their headquarters. As we drove towards a small bridge I was happy to discover a 2nd Armored tank, but I was disgusted because the tank was blocking the bridge across a small stream. A grey-haired sergeant was in the turret of the tank. I judged that it was a World War I sergeant who could be as stubborn as he was old. According to the war game rules, armored tanks were not permitted to use any bridge. Tanks had to cross or ford the streams in the water. If the tank could not ford the stream, the engineers had to build a pontoon bridge. In war it was assumed that all bridges would be destroyed. I would read the rules to the Army sergeant and get him off the bridge!

Cooling my anger, I reasoned that before I ordered the sergeant off the bridge I should try to learn where the 2nd Armored Headquarters was located. If I made the sergeant angry, he would refuse to tell me anything. As I approached the bridge I saw that a second tank was submerged in the water on the side of the bridge. Only the turret of the tank was out of the water. I studied the sunken tank as I approached the bridge.

"She's in deep!" a high pitched voice called. "The men were able to get out!"

The old army sergeant put on his helmut, and I saw two silver stars! Going into shock, I could see two silver stars on the tank! It was Gen. Patton who had called to me!

"Yes, sir!" I froze in place.

"Their speed was not high enough when they hit the water. I'm sure they could float all the way across the stream if they had hit the water at top speed! We gotta be able to cross this kind of stuff without bridges. It takes too much time to build a pontoon bridge for these little streams.

"Yes, sir!"

Gen. Patton continued to explain the proper way to maneuver a tank. Finally, he asked, "What outfit you with?"

"I Armored Corps, sir."

"Where in hell is the G-4? The Supply Officer? Where in hell is my gas? I need gas! I understand it's a hundred miles away." Gen. Patton continued to ask questions. At last, he called our former Supply Officer by name and asked if I knew what the colonel planned to do about the gasoline problem.

I answered, "He does not plan to do anything, sir."

"Then this war game is over! I cannot move ten miles without gas." He continued to stress his need for gasoline. Finally, he asked if I knew where the former G-4 Officer could be reached.

"He cannot be reached, sir. He is on his way to Fort Knox."

"Then who in hell is the G-4, for I Armored Corps?"

"I am, sir."

There was silence as Gen. Patton stared at me in amazement. He mumbled profanity and disappeared into his tank. I turned away and walked to my staff car. It was easy to see that Gen. Patton was disgusted with such a junior officer. I was disgusted that I had not been permitted to explain where the gas was located.

Before I reached the staff car, Gen. Patton called, "Lieutenant!"

I turned to see him jump from the tank with a bundle of maps in his hand.

"I am Gen. Patton. I am the Commanding General of the 2nd Armored Division. We need gas. Lots of gas! What's your name?"

I gave him my name.

Gen. Patton started with simple facts. "We've got a real problem here."

He spread his maps on the trunk of the staff car. Pointing on the map, he said, "This is where we expect Gen. Drum to be with the First Army. Our problem is we have to cross this stream, that river, and try to get into position for a battle in this area. But the problem is we do not have gas."

When I had a chance to speak, I said, "General, in the Armored Corps we do not have trucks, tank trucks, cans, nor men to move a hundred gallons of gas. There is no possible way that we could supply gas on the route which you have pointed out on the map. I am sorry to say that the only place we can get gasoline to you is here. I pointed to the railroad where the tank cars were parked on the tracks. We could not find the exact location on Gen. Patton's map.

"General, please let me show you on my maps where the gas is available." I reached in the car for my maps. My driver was sitting as stiff as a mummy. Everyone was rigid when Gen. Patton was near.

As I unfolded my maps, Gen. Patton asked, "Where did you get that map?"

"From National Geographic."

"How?"

"I subscribe to the magazine. The maps come with the magazine."

Studying the map, he commented, "Your map is a hell of a lot better than mine! I have been using gas station maps! All of my military maps are out of date."

We compared maps. I was anxious to explain the facts about the location of the railroad tank cars but did not have a chance. I was a new military officer, but I knew that two star generals were not interrupted.

Gen. Patton continued to present the problem. "Knowing the railroads I doubt that they would move the gas for a week. We need that gas now. Even if we could get the gas there...we are dry! But we could send trucks for a

16

few hundred gallons...but we couldn't get out any gas from a tank car. All of this might be in violation of the rules for our war games."

Gen. Patton paused and smiled, "But if...!"

It was my turn to smile! "General Patton, the gas is on the tracks right there now." I pointed to the marks I had made on the map. "It is not in violation of the rules for the war games. Our Corps Chief of Staff checked this out with the umpires."

"But that railhead is off the main highways where we had planned our attack! Lieutenant, whose idea was it to move that gas by rail? Do you know that the tank cars are there and going to stay there?"

"I just came from there! The railroad will not move the tank cars. I had the task of getting the gas to you and that was the only place I could see that we could make it available. I have been assured that the tank cars will not be moved for a week."

"It can't be! The war games do not start until midnight tonight. You broke the rules by moving too early!"

"General, if it is in violation, it is not your fault because our Chief of Staff cleared everything for me. That gas can be considered gas which you could capture from the enemy!"

"Can we just go up there and tank-up? Are you sure we will not get in trouble with the umpires?

I explained the clearance with the umpires, the gravity feed plan, the contract with the railroad, and all of the facts which I had on the tank cars.

Gen. Patton took my map and spread it out on the top of the staff car. He was tall enough to use the top of the four-door sedan. I continued to hold the other maps on the trunk. He drummed his fingers on the top of the car and mumbled, "No one would ever expect us to take a longer route. It is further, but we will have plenty of gas. We will send a light force...They should be able to return with enough to...In six hours.."

WE CAN ALWAYS LEARN FROM EACH OTHER

Gen. Patton turned to me, "You son-of-a-bitch! We can sure learn from each other! May I borrow your map? My old friend, Gen. Drum, will not even have a map showing where I am going to attack! Gen. Drum is the Commanding General of the Army against us, you know. He is an old friend, but I sure as hell would enjoy capturing him."

I agreed to loan my map. Requests by a two-star general were not denied by a lieutenant.

He gave me his gas station maps, saying, "Not a fair trade, but we gotta move fast. Would you wait right here for a minute while I cross this stream? I want to be sure that our tanks can cross this kind of water without a pontoon bridge. Then, if I may, I would like to hitch-hike a ride with you back to headquarters. I have to get back as fast as possible to make a change in our battle plan!"

As we walked towards the bridge and Gen. Patton's tank, he said, "We can always learn from each other. You watch me cross this stream. You taught me that you reserve officers can solve problems. Let me show you how to get a tank across a river!"

GENERAL PATTON'S WAR FACE

OBSERVATION HILL FOR DESERT MANEUVERS

GENERAL PATTON PREACHING THE PRINCIPLES
(note cavalry boots)

ASSUMING COMMAND OF I ARMORED CORPS

WAR MAP FOR CAROLINA WAR GAMES
(note cavalry boots)

GENERAL PATTON AS THE CHEER LEADER

EVERY NEW GENERAL RECEIVES A GUN SALUTE
(note one hundred foot flag pole in background)

LIGHT TANKS <u>WILL</u> CROSS SMALL RIVERS

ALWAYS DO EVERYTHING YOU EXPECT OF THE MEN YOU COMMAND

Gen. Patton jumped onto the side of his tank and squeezed into the turret. The tank driver "buttoned up," closing the front window of the tank so that water and bullets could not enter. When the driver was buttoned up, the man in the turret controlled the direction of the tank by pressure on the right or left shoulder of the driver. The pressure on the driver's shoulder was made with the foot of the man in the turret. The speed of a turn was determined by the degree of the pressure of the foot on the shoulder. Hard pressure on the right shoulder meant a hard right turn. This was not a good system, but the best we had been able to devise in 1941. The driver had a tiny periscope which he could use when he was buttoned up. This tiny periscope had a field of vision which was small. Most of the time the man in the turret would be in control of the tank.

Gen. Patton's head popped out of the turret. The armored tank backed off the bridge and into the weeds in the roadside ditch. When the tank had backed about a hundred yards from the bridge, the driver raced his engine to full speed. Gen. Patton braced his body against the iron side of the turret. The tank tracks started throwing dirt into the air and headed for the river. There was a great splash as the tank hit the water. The engine sputtered, and I was sure there would be a wet general crawling out of the tank. The silver stars on the general's flag disappeared under the water. For a moment the tank floated on the water until the tank's tracks jammed into the mud on the other side of the stream. The engine continued to sputter, but the tank rolled up the bank. When the tank stopped, mud and water dripped from every nut and bolt. Gen. Patton's head disappeared again as he went into the tank. Suddenly he was out of the tank and running to my car.

I would learn later that Gen. Patton had follow d one of his basic principles: "Always do everything you expect of the men you command." A slow attack on the river with a

A COMMANDER WILL COMMAND

When Gen. Patton assumed a command there was an instant change throughout the entire organization. The command changed as if every man was changed from 110 volt motivation to 440! Executive managers and psychologists lecture on how to exercise authority and to achieve upmanship. Gen. Patton did not follow many of the usual principles of management. Psychologists would complain that Gen. Patton's principles failed to protect the ego of the man. Gen. Patton would answer that a dead soldier did not have any ego. Everything Gen. Patton did was to prevent his soldiers from being killed so they could kill the enemy.

I remember Gen. Patton assuming command of I Armored Corps. It was Jan. 15, 1942, a few weeks after Pearl Harbor on December 7. I Armored Corps was bivouacked in a pine tree grove on the edge of the main post of Fort Benning, Georgia after our move from Ft Knox Our I Armored Corps was a hybrid military organization. Fort Benning was a standard-brand type of military organization, an infantry post. The I Armored Corps was a collection of men from infantry, field artillery and cavalry organizations. In simple terms, the armored tanks did the work of the foot soldiers, used the big guns of the field artillery, and raced into combat at speeds that exceeded the speed of horses. Although Hitler was using tanks to destroy Europe, many of our infantry, field artillery, and cavalry officers were not ready to let any new tank outfit take over their duties despite Hitler's success with tanks.

There was a dream among the cavalrymen that there would be a day when horses would return. Many of these horse-thinking officers held high positions of command in Washington. No tank outfit would be permitted to change the established military trunk-to-tail thinking of who would get the command positions to win the war.

Because we were a hybrid organization with our noisy tanks, we were removed from the main post area. Another reason for us to be off the main post was that our track-laying tanks could destroy roads. In our off-post area, our headquarters building looked like a small chicken house for laying hens. We lived in tents and used the pot-bellied stoves from World War I for heating our tents and our headquarters building.

We received orders from Washington that Gen. Patton would assume command of our I Armored Corps on the 15th day of January, 1942. No hour of the day was indicated on the order. Usually a new commanding general would arrive some time after the date of assuming the command and stroll into headquarters after he and his wife moved their clothes and property into military quarters. All of our quarters were in tents including the quarters for the Commanding General. Wives did not come to our camp and did not stay in the area. The next day after receiving the notice that Gen. Patton would assume command, we received an order from General Patton! The Patton order gave the same date but set the exact hour that Gen. Patton would assume command of I Armored Corps. This second order provoked laughter from the older officers on the staff. It was unheard of for a new commander to set an exact hour for assuming command. Knowing Gen. Patton, some of the older officers asked for and secured transfers to other organizations rather than serve under Gen. Patton.We younger officers were not excited because we had served under several new commanding Generals. There was such a great need for officers of all ranks that a new general was as common as a new truck or tank.

The morning that Gen. Patton was to assume command I started working without remembering that it was the day that Gen. Patton was to arrive. As a first Lieutenant I would not have any military function nor duty assignment for the new commander. In a few days I would be asked for reports on my area of work.

ALWAYS DO EVERYTHING YOU EXPECT OF THE MEN YOU COMMAND

In 1976, thirty-five years after the Carolina maneuvers, I was watching a television interview of one of FDR's top advisors. I had forgotten about this gas problem until I heard FDR's advisor comment, "The Carolina maneuvers of 1941 kept Gen. Drum from a high command in World War II. He was in line for Eisenhower's job. Gen. Patton captured Gen. Drum on the first day of the war game. Drum accused Patton of buying gas from the local gas stations with Patton's own money. Gen. Drum never recovered from the public exposure of his capture. I think he retired after he lost the Carolina war game in front of all of the photographers."

Gen. Patton would not have hesitated to have purchased gas from local stations with his own money if it had been possible, but heavy armored tanks could not use the roads to get to local gas stations. No gas station would have had enough gas for a division of armored tanks.

As I listened to the television interview, I remembered again our suspicions of 1941 that the political military leaders had planned to make Gen. Patton and the tanks appear worthless in war. Their plan had failed.

Within a few days after the arrival of the I Armored Corps in Fort Knox, Kentucky, we were ordered to Fort Benning, Georgia. The 2nd Armored Division and Gen. Patton were stationed at Fort Benning. The rumors were getting stronger that Gen. Patton would be the new Commanding General of our I Armored Corps. Many on the staff were alarmed. Although my experience with Gen. Patton had put me in the hospital with a cold chill from exhaustion, I had enjoyed working with him.

CHAPTER 2

PRINCIPLES OF COMMAND AND MANAGEMENT

tank and it would sink in the mud. Within a few hours in the darkness of midnight, every tank of the 2nd Armored Division would charge across that little river.

On the drive to Gen. Patton's headquarters, he never gave a single instruction to my driver. I did not know which roads to take, but Gen. Patton would not give any orders to my driver. He would say, "Would you ask your driver to turn at the next road." I did not need to repeat the instruction! The driver obeyed! Gen. Patton would not break a command channel. I was in I Armored Corps which did not take any orders from the 2nd Armored Division. When we reached Gen. Patton's headquarters, he thanked me for the map and ran for his office tent.

When I reached our Corps Headquarters, I was ordered back in to the combat zone with a new driver. Drivers had to have sleep. Officers could sleep while staff cars were moving. I never found any unit of the 2nd Armored Division that night. The "Hell on Wheels" division was living up to its name. I spent Sunday driving from town to town trying to find Gen. Patton's headquarters.

Early Sunday afternoon Gen. Drum drove into the combat zone to have pictures taken for the newspapers and picture magazines. The war game was to last for ten days. Gen. Drum reasoned that the maneuvers would not get started until Monday morning. Sunday would be the day for both forces to prepare for the maneuvers on Monday. The picture taking was a disaster for Gen. Drum, but a field day for the photographers. As the photographers were shooting the action pictures of Gen. Drum giving orders and riding into "combat", an advance party of Gen. Patton's motorcycle riflemen roared into the area with all of their sirens screaming. Nothing in the war game rules made any exceptions for captured generals. Gen. Drum was treated as any other prisoner of war much to the enjoyment of the photographers. No amount of talking would move Gen. Patton's riflemen to release Gen. Drum.

I learned of Gen. Drum's capture from a telephone operator who had a soft southern accent. She told me she had talked with a Gen. Drum who wanted to be released from the prisoner of war camp. She said, "My, but that man was sure having a hissy-fit!"

Although the war game was over with the capture of Gen. Drum, I was busy day and night trying to get rations, supplies and gasoline relocated for the 2nd Armored Division. I changed from the staff car to a captured jeep. The jeep could go into the fields and wooded areas. Several nights later I returned to I Armored Headquarters completely exhausted. Our Chief of Staff complimented me, saying, "Keeping Gen. Patton happy is not an easy assignment!" I went to my tent and fell on my cot in a cold chill. With four blankets I could not stop shaking. Our Corps Surgeon checked on me and piled on more blankets. The shaking and the chill stopped, but the Corps Surgeon wanted a patient to put in his new ambulance. He strapped me on a litter, MASH style, and sent me to a permanent post hospital. I never returned to I Armored Corps in South Carolina. With the capture of Gen. Drum the maneuvers ended. Gen. Patton had set a clear record that tanks could win wars.

When I rejoined I Armored Corps in a new building at Fort Knox, Kentucky, it was Sunday afternoon and the radio was blaring something about enemy planes attacking Pearl Harbor. One of the senior officers on the staff said, "Those radio people will do anything to try to get people to listen to 'em."

Our intelligence officer suggested, "Gentlemen, we knew that a Jap task force was in the Pacific. That news must be correct. I am sure we will be at war!"

I would not see Gen. Patton again until he assumed the command of I Armored Corps. I had won Gen. Patton's confidence, and as a result I would be with him many times during the next year.

An hour before Gen. Patton's exact hour to assume command, we heard sirens screaming in the distance from the area of the main post at Fort Benning. The sirens were so loud that we were certain that several buildings were burning. All of our staff officers who had field glasses looked for smoke in the main post area.

One officer remarked, "The sound seems to be coming our way. We must have a grass fire!"

We walked around the area trying to determine the location of the fire. Suddenly a dozen motorcycles roared into our camp with their sirens screaming full blast. Every motorcycle rider was wearing a gleaming helmet with the insignia of the 2nd Armored Division, Gen. Patton's Hell on Wheels Division. Every man dismounted from his motorcycle and grabbed a polished rifle. They surrounded our building with rifles ready to fire! Not one of the riflemen spoke to us. I am sure that enemy troops would have shown more interest! It was half an hour before the time set for Gen. Patton to assume command.

One of our officers commented, "We sure must be in for something!"

We went inside our headquarters and tried to get back to work thinking this would be what Gen. Patton would want us to be doing when he arrived. Again we heard sirens in the distance. We could hear the rumble of heavy equipment and see clouds of dust rolling into the sky from track-laying equipment. It had to be that Gen. Patton was coming.

In advance of Gen. Patton were two light tanks with soldiers on top of the tanks. In the convoy with the tanks were two army trucks carrying more soldiers, and we were to discover they carried an American flag, the flag of I Armored Corps, and the flag of a two-star general. We had only one American flag in our area without any flag in front of our headquarters. When all the tanks and trucks were stopped in front of our building, the flags were posted in flag stands also furnished by the soldiers from the 2nd Armored Division. The flag posting ceremony was done with sharp commands and heel-clicking precision. All of the flags were covered. The soldiers formed a double line opposite our headquarters. Five of the soldiers remained with the flags. Every soldier was at rigid attention except for the automatic riflemen who were holding their rifles in position to fire. Every finger was on the trigger! By the time the ceremony of posting the flags in the flag stands was finished, all of the I Armored Corps staff were outside watching.

Our Chief of Staff said, "Perhaps we should try to get into some sort of military formation."

We lined up opposite the soldiers from Gen. Patton's 2nd Armored Division. There was a contrast in our military procedures and our appearance. Gen. Patton's soldiers lined-up by loud commands with every soldier snapping into position on command. We sauntered into a wavy line without any commands. We wore different uniforms. Some of our officers were in winter uniforms and some in part winter and part summer. Some of our officers insisted on wearing the insignia and shoulder patch of their old cavalry or field artillery units. Few of us had the insignia of the I Armored Corps. Some wore the overseas cap, the flat type; others wore the cap with the bill, the garrison type; some were without any headgear; one officer wore a campaign hat which was first used in the War with Spain! We whispered and talked with each other. Gen. Patton's men were so silent and stern that we stopped whispering.

Gen. Patton's men snapped into attention. We attempted to stand erect because coming into our area was a shiny World War II command car — two seats, no top, and a bar to give support while riding in a standing position in the back seat. Standing erect at the bar was Gen. Patton.

Our Chief of Staff said, "Perhaps we should try to get into some sort of military formation."

We lined-up opposite the soldiers from Gen. Patton's 2nd Armored Division. There was a contrast in our military procedures and our appearance. Gen. Patton's soldiers lined-up by loud commands with every soldier snapping into position on command. We sauntered into a wavy line without any commands. We wore different uniforms. Some of our officers were in winter uniforms and some in part winter and part summer. Some of our officers insisted on wearing the insignia and shoulder patch of their old cavalry or field artillery units. Few of us had the insignia of the I Armored Corps. Some wore the overseas cap, the flat type; others wore the cap with the bill; the garrison type; some were with out any headgear; one officer wore a campaign hat which was first used in the War with Spain! We whispered and talked with each other. Gen. Patton's men snapped into attention. We attempted to stand erect because coming into our area was a shiny World War II command car with two seats, no top, and a bar to give support while riding in a standing position in the back seat. Standing erect at the bar was Gen. Patton.

The General's command car stopped in front of the men from the 2nd Armored Division. Gen. Patton ignored us; not even a single glance in our direction. As he dismounted from the command car, one of our officers whispered, "Here comes a tear jerking speech!"

Gen. Patton approached his men, stopped, clicked his heels, and saluted. The Staff Sergeant was ready with a salute, and when both dropped their hands, Gen. Patton shouted "Dismissed!"

Gen. Patton continued to ignore us and walked to the front of our headquarters building. The five men standing by the covered flags were at rigid attention

The General spoke to the men, "Sergeant! Post the Colors!

Gen. Patton snapped into a salute, and held it as the men uncovered the bright new flags. Gen. Patton dropped his hand salute and ordered "Dismissed". He did a left-face, and marched toward us. In front of us, he did a rigid right-face. He did not salute nor speak. The soldiers of the 2nd Armored Division were driving away from our area. Most of the soldiers were sobbing under their shiny helmets.

Gen. Patton looked at his wrist watch. It was a few minutes before eleven! I am sure he was counting the seconds until eleven o'clock. His eyes did not meet ours. He gazed over our heads into the sky.

Suddenly he spoke, "I assume command of I Armored Corps! At ease!"

We placed our hands behind our backs and moved our left foot away from the right in a more restful position than attention. No one spoke. No one moved. Nothing like "Glad to be aboard," "Glad to be with you,!" "We are going to make a great team." None of these words.

Gen. Patton, still at attention, commenced, "We are in for a long war against a tough enemy. We must train millions of men to be soldiers. We must make them tough in mind and body, and they must be trained to kill. As officers we must give leadership in becoming tough physically and mentally. Every man in this command must be able to run a mile in fifteen minutes with a full military pack!"

One of our fat senior officers chuckled.

"Damn it!" Gen. Patton shouted, "I mean every man! Every officer, and enlisted man, staff and command; every man will run a mile! We will start running from this point in exactly thirty minutes! I will lead!"

Gen. Patton stopped speaking but his eyes moved slowly until he caught the eyes of every officer. The silence was so total the sun seemed to stop in the sky. The two stray dogs, always running around our area, stopped and remained motionless as if at attention awaiting Gen. Patton's command. There was no doubt in the minds of any man, nor in the minds of the two stray dogs, Gen. Patton was in command!

SUMMER SOLDIERS WILL BE TRANSFERRED
BEFORE THE SUN GOES DOWN

Before Gen. Patton dismissed us from our first confrontation, he announced, "I have in my hand the orders for the transfer of every officer in I Armored Corps. Every order is signed and dated today. Every officer wanting a transfer or refusing to run a mile will leave this command before the sun goes down!" Gen. Patton held a bundle of papers in his hands.

Gen. Patton was wearing what later I would learn was his war face. He shouted at us, "Those officers wanting to remain in I Armored Corps be back at this point in thirty minutes! Dismissed!"

It was a silent I Armored Corps staff that waited to speak until Gen. Patton was inside our headquarters building. One senior colonel said, "Gentlemen, it has been great working with all of you, but I am taking this opportunity to get out. Anybody want to go with me? I can get good assignments for anyone who wants to transfer to a new armored division which is being formed at Fort Knox."

The arguments commenced on the advantages and disadvantages of staying and leaving. As the youngest officer, no one asked me to transfer, and no one asked me to stay. From my Carolina experience with Gen. Patton, I could not see anything unreasonable in his demands. I knew I could not run a mile in fifteen minutes with a full military pack, because I did not have a full military pack Most of the staff had only bedding rolls.

As I waited for the full-pack run, I thought about Gen. Patton's harsh procedure of transferring every officer who wanted out of his command. How unlike the procedures I had learned in college courses on management. So many military and civilian executives assumed command with the words. "I will take a few months to learn the company policies and the people. I do not expect to make any great changes. I hope I can continue to follow the great traditions of this fine organization. We will try to stay on the same general course." All of such statements were supposed to unite the members of an organization. Gen. Patton attacked "summer soldiers" the first minute he was in command.

I rolled my bedding roll and strapped on my empty pistol holster. This was my full pack! No rifle, no ammunition, no canteen, almost nothing required to have a full military pack for a soldier. At exactly the time specified, Gen. Patton came to the porch of our headquarters to review his new staff. The war face was gone. He was smiling, "I do not see a full military pack among any of you so we will not run today! But get in shape! We will be doing a mile run every day! Let's all go over to the Fort Benning Officers Club and have lunch."

A general's desire was a command, so we met at the Officers' Club for lunch. By the time we arrived, Gen. Patton had arranged a round table for the exact number of men he knew would be present after the transfers. As I remember we had ten officers including Gen. Patton. The moment we were seated, Gen. Patton started his attack on the problems of I Armored Corps. He outlined his plans, set time limits on training, and scheduled every day of the week for a month. During the session Gen. Patton did not give any indication that he had ever seen me before. He never called me by name; all references were to G-4 which was my assigned office. I had the answers on the status of our arms and equipment.

Despite my having the answers, Gen. Patton announced that Col. Gay would be arriving to assume the duties of G-4 for the I Armored Corps, and that I would be Col. Gay's assistant. With this announcement, he called me by rank and not by name.

At a break in our afternoon meeting, one of our senior colonels congratulated me on being assigned as Assistant G-4 for the Corps. Being a civilian reserve officer, I asked, "Is that good? I thought I was being demoted from the position of acting G-4."

"Is that good? You are set for promotions as fast as the days go by! You could never expect to stay on as G-4 as a Lieutenant. That job cal's for a one star general. The Assistant G-4 calls for a full colonel. You are only a first Lieutenant. You will be holding a position four ranks above your present rank." The colonel was not jealous because he would soon have a general star. Although I was not serving in the Army for promotions, I was annoyed that Gen. Patton had not recognized me nor commented on the Carolina maneuvers.

Later in the week the General's Aide told me that I was to be at Gen. Patton's tent at seven in the evening. At this meeting we refought the battles of Carolina and laughed over the "captured" gas. He returned my National Geographic map! He told me about Col. Gay, when he would arrive, how much polo they had played together, and many of their experiences in the service.

A few days later, Col. Gay arrived to assume the work of the office of G-4. Col. Gay became Gen. Gay and was Gen. Patton's Chief of Staff during World War II. Col. Gay and I became close friends. It was Gen. Gay who was riding with Gen. Patton when Gen. Patton was killed in the auto accident in Germany.

Before Gen. Patton assumed command of I Armored Corps, we were a group of men shuffling papers trying to get the men and equipment to fill the assignments of an Armored Corps. The instant Gen. Patton assumed command, we were a team dedicated to one objective: kill the enemy. I thought of Tom Paine's words when Gen. Patton transferred every wavering officer. I am sure Gen. Patton knew the words, "These are the times that try men's souls. The summer soldier and the sunshine patriot will, in this crisis, shrink from the service of their country..."

These were the words Tom Paine had written during the dark days of the Revolutionary War in 1776.

KEEP A QUICK LINE OF COMMUNICATION

At one of our first staff meetings in January, 1942, Gen. Patton announced, "The war in Europe is over for us. England will probably fall this year. It is going to be a long war. Our first chance to get at the enemy will be in North Africa. We cannot train troops to fight in the desert of North Africa by training in the swamps of Georgia. I sent a report to Washington requesting a desert training center in California. The California desert can kill quicker than the enemy. We will lose a lot of men from heat, but the training will save hundreds of lives when we get into combat. I want every officer and section to start planning on moving all of our troops by rail to California."

In less than sixty days every I Armored Corps unit was enroute to Indio, California. Our final destination was a point in the middle of the desert near the town of Desert Center which in 1942 had a total population of nineteen people! We were two commands, I Armored Corps and The Desert Training Center.

Our headquarters was approximately sixty miles east of Indio, California. Radio reception in our tents was poor due to the long distance between our portable radios and the broadcasting stations in Palm Springs and Los Angeles. Gen. Patton's first concern was always the welfare of the troops so he purchased radio broadcasting equipment. The initial investment was with his own money! Our signal corps troops installed the radio broadcasting equipment. The station broadcasted only news and music. The radio station was a quick method of communicating with the troops. Gen. Patton wanted to talk to the troops as often as possible. At a staff meeting, he said, "This new station should save several weeks of training time. We can reach the troops, every one of them, as often as we need. In an emergency we could reach every man in seconds."

Our desert radio broadcasting station had one unusual feature. There was a microphone in Gen. Patton's office and a second microphone was by his bed in his tent. Day and night Gen. Patton could cut off all broadcasting and announce a special message or order from his personal mike When the music would click off we knew we would hear, "This is Gen. Patton!"

Often Gen. Patton would say, "I want every man to be alert tomorrow because we are doing the maneuvers for a lot of brass from Washington who don't know the first form thing about tanks or desert warfare. We must show them how wars can be won with speed. I am counting on every man."

The radio would click, and the music would return. There was no signing-off by Gen. Patton. He said what he wanted to say and clicked off. He did not hesitate in using the radio to remove any rank from command. Often his harsh words for an officer would provoke laughter from others. For example, one time Gen. Patton ordered, "Col. Blank, you are removed from command! If you know what is good for you, you will stay away from me for a week!"

The usual removal-from-command was accompanied with the order to appear before Gen. Patton immediately. There were many different reasons for removing officers. Usually it was because of a difference in training and strategy. Many National Guard and Reserve Officers had been trained only in defensive strategy. Gen. Patton did not believe in defending! He was always on the attack. Any officer who started following a strategy of "digging in" or preparing to defend was certain to be removed from command.

Gen. Patton used the radio to commend special efforts by the troops. He would announce, "Found a damn good soldier today!" He would continue giving the name of the man and the organization. When the officers knew they could be removed in an instant and the enlisted men knew they could be given special recognition by Gen. Patton, every man gave his best effort every hour of the day.

Every night Gen. Patton arranged a type of communication which united all soldiers. This communication seemed to unite us with the soldiers of history. Gen. Patton had the buglers blow Taps! Every organization down to a company of two hundred men had their own bugler. With twenty thousand men sleeping on the ground over a thirty mile strip of the desert valley, we had a hundred buglers.

A bugle for communication during the day in a tank outfit was as practical as a feather in a hail storm. No bugle call could be heard above the roar of the tanks and trucks but in the stillness of the night, a bugle call would carry for miles. With sound traveling at the rate of eleven hundred feet per second, it was impossible for all of the buglers to play Taps at the same time. It would take five seconds for the first note of the Headquarter's bugler to reach a bugler a mile away. Thus, with a hundred buglers blowing Taps at different places and times and with the echos bouncing off the mountains, it was a sound to cause the mind of every man to pause for a moment in prayer. Those bugle calls made us feel as if we were a part of an organization which had the power of the armies of the centuries.

No soldier could go to sleep after the last echo of the bugle call because the desert coyotes were impressed with the sounds and carried on coyote-conversation from every mountain range. The wails of the coyotes continued for a period of time longer than the bugles. Gen. Patton "put us to bed" with the pride of knowing that we were a part of a military organization which united all of the forces of Nature, including the coyotes.

I remember Gen. Patton saying one night, "I love that sound. It takes me back to my service in the Cavalry when I was an Aide to Gen. Pershing, in World War I."

PUNISHMENT FOR MISTAKES MUST BE IMMEDIATE OR A DEAD MAN DOES NOT HAVE ANY EGO

Gen. Patton's principles of discipline did not match modern rules for management. The idea of giving reprimands in a quiet and personal conversation to avoid hurt feelings was not for Gen. Patton.

I remember his words, "When you make a mistake in war, the punishment is death! The big trouble is that your mistake could cause a hundred men to die. No one ever hears, 'peek-a-boo' I see you. I am going to count to ten and then shoot! That's not the way war works. If the enemy can shoot first, you will be dead!"

In our staff meetings Gen. Patton advised instant punishment for every mistake. Often a staff member would go to the defense of a friend or suggest some form of soft punishment. When an officer with a degree in management would explain the newer ideas for leadership, Gen. Patton would explode, "All that 'save the ego business' is not for war. A dead man does not have any ego! How long after you touch a match does it take before you get burned? War follows the law of Mother Nature. What happens to the tree that does not put its roots down deep? Such a tree will die for lack of water or blow over with the first wind. Every mistake has its own punishment. How long does it take for a garden rake to hit you in the face when you step on the teeth turned toward you? Did you ever stub a toe on a rock? How long after you stub your toe until the pain comes?"

Every man serving with Gen. Patton knew that to make a mistake was to expect the wrath of his anger. It was not unusual to hear Gen. Patton's voice on the tank-command radio, "Col. Blank, you are removed from command immediately!"

Such sudden changes in command caused every man to give one hundred per cent of his effort every minute. Every time any man used the radio, he knew the Old Man could be listening. The term, Old Man, was not a term to discredit Gen. Patton. It meant love and devotion for a leader.

PUNISHMENT FOR MISTAKES MUST BE
IMMEDIATE OR
A DEAD MAN DOES NOT HAVE ANY EGO

Gen. Patton's bark on the radio was worse than his bite. After removing an officer from a command, Gen. Patton would order the officer to report to Headquarters. After a session with the officer, Gen. Patton would usually reinstate the officer's command. What Gen. Patton would do would depend, as he would say, on "Whether that officer learned anything from the demotion."

For all of us who had served on the staff for several months it was difficult to keep from laughing when a removed officer would protest his punishment. It was more fun for us when a new officer, transferred from Washington, would protest Gen. Patton's punishment. Gen. Patton would stare at the protesting officer for a moment as we staff officers would grin knowing that an explosion was coming. Gen. Patton would start slowly, "Colonel, what happens when you touch hot electric wires?"

The officer would answer, "You get shocked."

Gen. Patton would proceed as if he were leading a child. "How long after you touch the electric wires until you get shocked?"

"The shock would come instantly."

"Right again!" Gen. Patton would react as if the Washington officer was displaying outstanding intelligence. "Now that time span from the touch and the shock is exactly what we try to do with our training for war. A mistake in war can cause instant death. We are training for war, colonel. We cannot save the ego of any man when the punishment is death. For his mistake we cannot delay punishment for mistakes. Do you understand, colonel? War is a killing business?"

The colonel had the message.

Gen. Patton would continue," I cannot kill a man in our combat training, but I can make every man wish to be dead rather than take the wrath of my anger!"

PUNISHMENT FOR MISTAKES MUST BE
IMMEDIATE OR
A DEAD MAN DOES NOT HAVE ANY EGO

There would be a long silence as Gen. Patton would walk back and forth in front of the room. Every man knew that if a mistake was made Gen. Patton's wrath would strike with the speed of lightning

"There is only one kind of discipline — Perfect Discipline. If you do not enforce and maintain discipline, you are potential murderers!"Gen. Patton left the area, but his message stayed with us.

SAY WHAT YOU MEAN AND
MEAN WHAT YOU SAY

Men cannot be excited to kill by soft words spoken in an uncertain voice. When Gen. Patton spoke, every man knew exactly what was demanded. Gen. Patton would explain, "It takes a lot of talking to get out American young men ready to kill, to murder. Killing is against their nature. The language of war is not polite. War is hell. It is difficult to make our fine American youth understand that the enemy wants to kill him. We have to work hard to keep our men from being killed. We have to work even harder to get them ready to kill. Swearing helps to get the point across. When I give a command and put in enough profanity, the soldiers will understand. I use the language of soldiers who are ready to kill. They know what I mean! Another thing, I always wear a war face. There dare not be any smiling when you give orders. War is not as smiling business. I'll shoot anyone of you who ever has his picture taken with a smile on his face."

Whenever he would give the "war face" orders, I thought of the Indians who painted their faces for war. Gen. Patton did not miss a trick in preparing troops for war.

With profanity Gen. Patton secured the objective of always communicating with the troops. There is a difference in the soft words, "In the morning, weather permitting, we may attack the enemy, I guess," and Gen. Patton's type of order, "At exactly five in the morning we are going out and kill every damn one of those sons-of-bitches!"

With all of the profanity, many assumed that Gen. Patton was always in a fit of anger. His fits of rage were his training methods to excite the troops. An angry soldier is more dangerous than a smiling soldier. After Gen. Patton's fits of anger before the troops he would return for a staff meeting and be as calm as a church elder and ask whether or not the troops received the message.

There was one time that Gen. Patton went into a rage over his own mistake. One night he dropped his turned-on flashlight through one of the holes of our six-hole latrine. The pit of the latrine was several feet below the seats, and the flashlight continued to glow for several hours. It was a most unusal sight to enter the latrine in the middle of the night and see the soft indirect lighting from the six seats.

Gen. Patton's anger or disgust continued into the morning briefing session of the staff. He said, "I am the idiot that let his flashlight roll into the latrine. Put the cost of that flashlight on a charge sheet to me. I do not want the loss of that flashlight charged off as a battle casualty!"

Everyone laughed. Playing with the idea, he said, "On second thought, I have a couple of officers I know that are better qualified at digging out that flashlight than they are at leading troops. I may assign them to digging out that flashlight."

No one knew what officers were in line for the assignment of salvaging the flashlight. Every man who heard the story tried harder to avoid Gen. Patton's assignment of digging in the latrine.

After the first few days of hearing Gen. Patton swear, his profanity did not seem to be swearing. When Gen. Patton asked God to damn something, somehow it seemed to us that God would obey! Certainly we knew that if God did not listen, Gen. Patton would cause no end of trouble. Gen. Patton's relationship with God was as if two old friends were showing their friendship by using words of abuse. Gen. Patton was fighting for God! God should cooperate! His prayer for fair weather for fighting is an example:

"Almighty and most Merciful Father, we humbly beseech Thee to restrain these immoderate rains, grant us fair weather for battle, graciously hearken to us as soldiers who call upon Thee, that armed with Thy Power, we may advance unto victory and establish Thy justice among men and nations." Gen. Patton expected God to get the message.

SAY WHAT YOU MEAN AND
MEAN WHAT YOU SAY

Gen. Patton meant everything he said, and he said it in a manner that left no doubt about what he was saying. It was common for some freshman news reporter to ask, "Gen. Patton, may I quote you in my paper on what you just said?"

The General would answer in disgust, "You can quote me anywhere you like on every damn word! If I had not meant what I said, I would not have said it."

ANY MAN WHO THINKS HE IS INDISPENSABLE, AIN'T

Gen. Patton did not use "ain't" in his usual conversation. "Ain't" seemed to make this principle strike with greater speed especially when seasoned with profanity. Gen. Patton would explain, "In war every man is expendable. That includes me! Especially me! Any man who starts thinking he is indispensable already isn't worth his weight in anything. I will get rid of such an officer immediately. Every man must be willing to give his life for others to accomplish a mission, but don't lose your life without making several of the enemy lose theirs. Don't die alone. Take several of the enemy with you!"

He would continue, "Any man who starts thinking he is indispensable will start staying from the front. He will spend more time in the rear eschelons thinking he is too important to risk his life at the front where the shells are falling. That man is a double coward or a coward twice over. He is afraid of himself and of the enemy. In war every man is expendable."

Gen. Patton transferred officers because of their overestimation of their importance. I remember one officer who qualified for a transfer in a few short minutes. In the desert we had a two hour break during the hottest time of the day. Our mail would arrive during this extremely hot period. Usually only one junior grade officer would walk in the sun to pick up the mail for all of the staff. One day a captain announced that he was going to the mail room and a dozen officers asked to have their mail returned. The captain never returned with the mail! Later, in the mess tent we asked the captain what happened to our mail.

The captain, speaking as seriously as a minister announcing a death, said, "Gentlemen, when I picked up my mail I found my letter of promotion to the rank of Major. I did not deem it proper for a field grade officer to be carrying mail for junior grade officers."

ANY MAN WHO THINKS HE IS INDISPENSABLE, AIN'T

We were so shocked we could not laugh! It was too crazy to believe. Just as Gen. Patton had advised, "Any man who thinks he is so all-important already isn't." This officer lost all of his value for the I Armored Corps the instant he received his promotion.

As our I Armored Corps and Desert Training Center grew in numbers, our staff became more specialized in duties. Every officer had a specific responsibility and the proper amount of authority to get the job done. In addition we were supposed to know about the activities of all of the other sections. This sharing of information was the principle reason for many of our staff meetings.

Gen. Patton would advise, "We can expect that some of us will be killed. We do not want the loss of one man to stop our killing the enemy. Always have a man trained and ready to take over in case you are killed. The test of your success is whether you could be killed and nothing would be lost!"

In civilian life this principle is not followed too frequently. Many corporate executives all the way down the line to the janitors strive to prove their worth by trying to be indispensable. It is a type of job security to keep others from knowing the work operation. Gen. Patton demanded that every man be expendable to win every battle. He did not spare himself. He repeated so often, "I do not know of a better way to die than to be facing the enemy. I pray that I will fall forward when I am shot. That way I can keep firing my pistols! I was shot in the behind in World War I! I do not want to be hit there again. I got a medal for charging at the enemy, but I have had to spend a lot of time explaining how I got shot in the behind! I want to fall forward!"

ANY MAN WHO THINKS HE IS INDISPENSABLE
AIN'T

When I first heard Gen. Patton make these remarks about how he wanted to die in combat, I was sure that he was building courage for the men. As I knew him better I was sure that he fully intended to ignore all risks with the hope of being killed leading his troops into combat. When he said, "Every man is expendable - especially me," he meant every word.

THE MISSION IS ALL IMPORTANT!
THINK ABOUT STANDARD RULES LATER

One afternoon Gen.Marshall was inspecting our Desert Training Command. It seemed as if all of the officers in the Pentagon were with Gen. Marshall. We were on an observation point which we called "Patton's Nose." That is, we called it "Patton's Nose" when we knew he could not hear us. He knew that the troops called it, Patton's Nose." He wanted it called, "The Head!" Through field glasses we were watching the movement of the tanks several miles away. From the little hill we could see for over seventy miles in the desert. We had erected two large wall tents to provide shade for the high ranking visiting officers from Washington. The Signal Corps had installed a public address system which was connected with the radio network of the tank commanders so the radio commands of the combat units could be heard on the public address system. As we watched the dust swirl into the air miles away, Gen. Patton would break into the radio chatter to explain to the visiting officers the strategy of the attack.

Gen. Patton announced, "Now that the blue force has located the red enemy, the light tanks will go around the right flank and destroy the red enemy from the rear." There were questions from the visiting officers and discussions about speed of movement and tank capabilities.

Time elapsed and no light tanks moved around the right flank. The desert settled into total calm! No dust was stirring into the air. The wind blew the swirling dust into oblivion. Nothing was moving except Gen. Patton's anger. Being close to him, I could hear him call on first one channel and then another in an attempt to reach the light tank commander.

Suddenly, Gen. Patton announced, "We have had a mix-up in commands. This is exactly how battles are lost in war. This maneuver is called off until tomorrow morning. I can assure everyone that this mix-up will not happen tomorrow."

Gen. Patton asked all of his staff to gather around him and ordered an immediate staff meeting with the tank commanders. The task of the staff was to round-up the tank commanders and get them to the meeting. At the staff meeting Gen. Patton related the plans for the demonstration battle for the Washington officers. He explained where the mix-up had happened which caused the failure of the mission for the blue force. The failure was pinpointed on the light tank commander, a young lieutenant. After the discussion and the evaluations of the actions, Gen. Patton called the young lieutenant to the front of the staff.

"Lieutenant, you know the need for speed and fast action. You were in command of the light tank task force. But where were you? Why didn't you attack? And what radio channel were you on? Why couldn't I reach you on the radio? Why did you fail to answer?" Gen. Patton was trying to be calm. "We are all interested in your explanation, Lieutenant."

The young lieutenant was nervous but he spoke with conviction, "General, I am under the command of Col. Blank. I knew I was supposed to attack, and we were ready. We were on a radio channel which Col. Blank ordered us to use so that our commands would be secret — so the enemy would not hear what we were doing. Col. Blank told me not to move until he gave the order. I never received the order to attack!"

Gen. Patton asked "What's your explanation, Col. Blank?"

"Our radio went dead, Gen. Patton," the colonel answered.

"Then you should have dashed over there on your two damn feet! Radios will always be going dead! We must be ready for such radio break-downs."

Gen. Patton slapped his leg with his horse cavalry riding stick which he frequently used as a black board pointer. He looked into the desert. I knew he was trying to cool his anger."

"Col. Blank, I want to see you in my office immediately after this meeting is dismissed!"

Again Gen. Patton walked back and forth in front of the staff with a couple of slaps of his stick on the back of his leg. It was so silent that the slapping of his boot sounded like the explosion of a firecracker. The young lieutenant was standing at rigid attention.

Gen. Patton put his arm around the lieutenant saying, "Relax, Lieutenant! What you did was exactly right according to Army Regulations. But let me tell you something, if you want to be a Napoleon, think of the mission first! Forget about Army Regulations. Army Regulations are written by those who have never been in battle. They write about what they have been told by others. Our only mission in combat is to win. If we do not win, you can forget everything! After the battles are over, those in the Pentagon can write about what we did wrong!

So often I remember Gen. Patton advising, "Let the American soldier know what has to be done, and he will do it. Battles are won by determined soldiers who do not spend a split second trying to remember what Army Regulations had to say about what you should do when you are being shot at!"

ALWAYS BE ALERT TO
THE SOURCE OF TROUBLE

Gen. Patton was constantly checking with the troops to make sure they understood the mission. He spent every day and many nights training the troops. I was riding with him one evening at dusk when we were outside our diamond shaped defense. With desert combat there is no front combat area and rear eschelon for supplies and medical tents. A desert command is the same as a battle ship sailing on the ocean. The enemy can attack from any direction. The guns of a battle ship cannot be turned to fire into the ship, but the guns of our tanks could be turned to fire into our own troops. With noise and confusion, the troops could get excited and forget the location of our own headquarters, the center of the diamond shaped defense area. We chained the guns to fire in only one direction, and we used aiming stakes but nothing was successful. Any morning after a scare from an enemy attack at night and the guns on our tanks could be aimed directly at the center of our own camp. We wanted to prevent the slaughter of our own troops when we reached actual combat and used live ammunition.

Gen. Patton and I were driving in what would have been enemy territory if we had been in combat. We drove towards our own camp when we saw one of the outer guards. Gen. Patton asked me to approach the guard to make sure the guard knew his exact duty assignment.

I walked towards the guard who stopped me with the order of "Halt!" His automatic rifle was aimed directly at me. I gave the correct pass word and he told me I could advance. I asked the guard what his duties were. He gave a correct report of his duty assignment.

I continued, "From which direction do you expect trouble?"

The guard pointed to the center of our camp!

I started to discipline him, "That is the center of our camp. The enemy would be in the opposite direction. You pointed to the exact center of our camp!"

ALWAYS BE ALERT TO
THE SOURCE OF TROUBLE

He put me in my place, "You did not ask anything about the enemy. I know where the enemy is! You asked where I expected trouble. I expect trouble from right back there! That's Gen. Patton's headquarters! That's where I expect trouble!"

I could hear Gen. Patton laughing. He called to me, "Come on back, Williamson. That man understands his mission."

The guard asked, "Who was that?"

I answered, "That was Gen. Patton."

"My God!" the guard exclaimed, "You gotta expect Gen. Patton from all directions!"

Gen. Patton was chuckling when I climbed into the open command car. He commented, "We are doing better! We are up to the training level of the Roman legions!"

Since I did not have any knowledge of the training of the Roman legions I could not comment. Many years later I was reading the Gibbon's book, **The Decline and Fall of the Roman Empire**. I thought of Gen. Patton's words when I read, "It was an inflexible maxim of Roman displine, that a good soldier should dread his officers far more than the enemy."

SELECT LEADERS FOR ACCOMPLISHMENT AND NOT FOR AFFECTION

Any man who constantly flattered Gen. Patton would be transferred. Gen. Patton demanded obedience but not blindness. He never objected to an argument. He would not be angry at any man who spoke out on a valid point of difference.

I remember Gen. Patton telling about his method of selecting leaders. He would say, "Doesn't make any difference what rank. Could be for a promotion to the rank of colonel or sergeant. Picking the right leader is the most important task of any commander. I line up all of the candidates and give them a problem. I say, 'Men, I want a trench dug behind warehouse number ten. Make this trench eight feet long, three feet wide and six inches deep.' That's all I tell them! I use warehouse number ten because I know it has knot holes in the wall. While the candidates are checking their tools out at the warehouse, I get inside and watch them through the knot holes. The men will puzzle over why I want such a shallow trench. They will argue over whether six inches is deep enough for a gun emplacement. Others will complain that such a trench should be dug with power equipment. Others will gripe that it is too hot or too cold to dig. If the men are above the rank of lieutenant, there will be complaints that they should not be seen doing such lowly labor as digging a trench. Finally, one man will order, 'What difference does it make what that old SOB wants to do with this trench. Let's get it dug and get out of here.'"

Gen. Patton would pause before explaining, "That man will get the promotion. Never pick a man because he slobbers all over you with kind words. Too many commanders pick dummies for their staff. These dummies don't know how to do anything except say, 'Yes.' Such men are not leaders. And any man who picks a dummy cannot be a leader. Pick the man who can get the job done!"

SELECT LEADERS FOR ACCOMPLISHMENT AND NOT FOR AFFECTION

I remember Gen. Patton saying so often, "Do I care whether the men like me? We are fighting a war. It is a killing business. I have to teach the troops how to protect themselves and to kill the enemy. I am not running for public office!"

EVERY LEADER MUST HAVE THE AUTHORITY
TO MATCH HIS RESPONSIBILITY

"If you run into any problem, tell them I sent you. You are acting for me. I will back you up all the way. Right or wrong, I will back you up! But you better be right!" Gen. Patton used these words in sending staff members to Washington or to other commands. He wanted total loyalty from his staff, and he gave total support to every staff member. We all knew that he would "back us up" even if we made a mistake. This "back up" caused every member to exert every effort to be right.

This is a basic principle of management. It is expressed as, "Never send a boy to do a man's job. The job may require the authority of a man, but the commander only gives the authority of a boy. It is easy to see the mistakes of asking heavy responsibilities without giving enough authority."

Gen. Patton would instruct, "Don't fire a rifle at a tank! Use a tank weapon on a tank! If you cannot make a kill, don't waste your ammo!"

This basic principle was violated by the politicians in the Gen. Patton face-slapping incident. Gen. Patton had the responsibility of winning the battles of the war, but he was not given the authority to discipline troops who retreated to the hospital to avoid combat. He was deeply concerned about the men in the hospitals. When one man said he was in the hospital without any injury, saying, "I just can't take combat!" Gen. Patton struck. We had been told many times that we would be shot if we turned away from the enemy! The Washington political leaders decided that Gen. Patton did not have any authority to slap a soldier. We, the American people, were lost in a sea of confusion over authority and responsibility. We were not up to the level of the Roman Legions who were trained to fear their commanders more than the enemy!

Ten years after this face slapping, the same soldier was interviewed at his home in Indiana. He commented to the news reporter, "The General (Patton) was a soldier. I never did like war and being overseas. Maybe I was dumb back there in Sicily. Some of the higher-ups were scared of their own jobs. Maybe if I had handled it right, I could have gotten home a lot sooner." This confession speaks for itself! Gen. Patton hated this type of man. In the earlier years of our history, such a man could have been shot. This is the type of soldier that could cause thousands to be killed for his failure to accept his responsibility.

I remember Gen. Patton telling us. "You can turn away from the enemy, but you better be in a prone position — on a hospital litter. The Washington political leaders did not give Gen. Patton the "back-up" which he needed to discipline the troops for combat. I am glad that Gen. Patton died before he could hear the Washington political leaders comment about the war in Viet Nam, "A little bit of war someplace in the world is good for the economy of the United States!" Such a statement indicated that the authority to win the war did not match the responsibility. The responsibility to the United States was not to win the war but to help the political economy! Gen. Patton did not hesitate to ask every man to die for his country, but he would never ask any man to die for the economy of the country.

PROTECT THE TROOPS FIRST
THE WISHES OF SUPERIOR OFFICERS
ARE SECONDARY

This Patton Principle is the opposite of the usual rule, "Obey all orders no matter what." It does not match the military rule of "Ours is not to reason why, ours is to do or die." This Patton principle also violated some of Gen. Patton's principles of loyalty. But no officer ever suffered Gen. Patton's anger if a valid reason existed for differing with the General. I know. I differed with him many times but never without reasons. He did demand absolute loyalty when time would not permit discussion.

We had not been in our desert training center a month when Gen. Marshall wanted to move all of the troops to North Africa to engage in combat withthe Germans. We were not ready. Every day Gen. Patton would rage at the troops. Every night we posted guards as if we were in combat, but we were not ready for combat with the enemy when we could not combat the heat of the desert. Gen. Patton worked at the training. I remember his shouting at the truck drivers, "I will shoot any man that drives his truck within two hundred yards of another truck. Get in the habit of staying apart. Make the enemy waste his ammunition on only one vehicle. Never let the enemy get two sitting ducks. Never let the enemy get two trucks with one shot. Make the enemy make a separate attack on every truck. You will have a chance to live longer!"

We were in the middle of a morning staff meeting when Gen. Marshall called from Washington. Gen. Patton took the call in front of the staff. We could hear only his side of the conversation, "It takes at least six weeks to get a man ready to be a soldier in the desert. Anything short of six weeks, and we will lose more men from heat than from the enemy." Gen. Patton stressed the argument with multiple words of profanity.

Gen. Patton won the argument over his old friend, Gen. Marshall, the Chief of Staff for all of our Armies. Gen. Patton and Gen. Marshall were good friends, but friends or not, to swear at the Chief of Staff could be the death of a military career. Gen. Patton never placed his military

PROTECT THE TROOPS FIRST
THE WISHES OF SUPERIOR OFFICERS
ARE SECONDARY

career above his concern for the troops. Gen. Marshall was being pushed by Churchill to send troops to North Africa.

Gen. Patton did not know any half-way measure. No soldier could be "half-way" ready to kill the enemy. He wanted the troops fully trained physically and mentally to kill. I remember his words, "We are going to move and move fast. We are not going to dig fox holes and wait for the enemy to come shootin' at us. When every soldier can move a mile with his rifle in fifteen minutes, we will confuse the hell out of them. They will waste their ammunition on their own people. We will always be where the enemy never expects us to be!"

Gen. Patton caused Gen. Marshall to slow down the movement of the troops into combat. Gen. Patton would rage, "It's a damn waste of the most wonderful manhood of America to send green troops into combat before they are ready. We must be trained to win."

As usual, Gen. Patton was right, but he was a lone-thinker. The history of World War II indicates that this principle was broken often, but always with the fate of losing "the most wonderful manhood of America."

CHAPTER 3

PRINCIPLES FOR GOOD HEALTH

AN ACTIVE MIND CANNOT EXIST
IN AN INACTIVE BODY

"Wars are won by men with strong wills and strong bodies!" Gen. Patton preached.

"A strong will to win is more important than a strong body! Men have won battles when totally exhausted and near death from injuries. However, that will to win did not get into the brain without first having a strong body. You have to keep the body active to keep all of the juices running to the right places." Gen Patton never stopped stressing physical fitness.

In the winter of 1941, we were stationed at Ft. Benning, Georgia. We were the I Armored Corps, the first corps of tanks in World War II. The term, corps, meant that we should have two or more tank divisions in our command. A tank division had approximately fifteen thousand men and approximately one hundred tanks of light and medium size. We had never seen a medium tank! We had pictures! Everything we did was based on guess-work because we did not have any guide on how many men or tanks would make up a corps. We did have some trucks and cars. Every piece of equipment we had was exactly the same as the civilian models on the highway. We were the I Armored Corps in name, but we were short fifty thousand men and all of the fighting equipment for war. Most of our guns were stove pipes.

In December after Pearl Harbor our primary task was to determine on paper exactly how many men and how many tanks should be in an armored corps. Every day we sent proposals to Washington indicating what we thought would be the correct number of men and tanks. We were already in the war, but we were working on the paper work to prepare the proper tables of organization and basic allowances for a corps. The method of organization was called, "TO," Table of Organization. The equipment list was called, "TBA," Table of Basic Allowances.

AN ACTIVE MIND CANNOT EXIST
IN AN INACTIVE BODY

Every day we received new TO's and TBA's from Washington. We had to study these charts and propose changes if we could not approve. Our approval was based on our experiences with the men and equipment in the field under combat conditions or as near combat conditions as we could create. For combat conditions we substituted trucks for tanks and eight inch stove pipes for large guns. The war was raging in Europe and in the Pacific, but we were still firing stovepipe guns.

Gen. Patton demanded that every man run a mile every day. This was thirty years before jogging became so popular. Most of my work was at a standard civilian desk and swivel chair. Frequently Gen. Patton would stop at my desk and ask, "How long you been sitting at that damn desk? Get up and get out of here! Check on the troops and the trucks! Your brain stops working after you sit in a swivel chair for twenty minutes. Keep moving around so the juices of the body will run to the right places, especially the brain! If you sit there too long all of the brain power will be in your shoes. You cannot keep your mind active when your body is inactive."

We filled every hour of the day with work, and Gen. Patton kept our bodies active!

BRAIN POWER COMES
FROM THE LUNGS

Gen. Patton did not order any man to stand erect, but he gave every man the reason for standing erect.

As I remember his advice he would say, "In war, as in everything else, a man needs all of the brains he can get. Nobody ever had too many brains. Brains comes from oxygen. Oxygen comes from the lungs where the air goes. This oxygen in the air gets into the blood and travels to the brain. Any fool can increase the size of his lungs by at least fifty per cent. Many can double their lung power. If you can double your lung power you could be twice as smart! Just breathe more air into your lungs. Take ten deep breaths several times a day. Take all the air you can get in and then hold it as long as you can. Air does not cost a dime! It takes brains to win wars and avoid the traps the enemy will set for us. Try this deep breathing and holding for ten seconds on each breath. Hold it until you pop! It will expand your lungs. Do this deep breathing when you are standing around wondering what to do. No reason for any man to be idle. He can always be doing something such as deep breathing. We are a bunch of lazy breathers. We use our lungs less and less so we increase our dumbness. Some of us smoke, like me. This cuts down on the power of the brain. But I don't smoke much. You breath deep — every one of you. We want every advantage we can get. We are going to kill the enemy because we will be smarter."

Gen. Patton did not order the staff not to smoke, but he did try to stop those that smoked excessively. All of his advice pertained to combat. I remember his saying, "You don't dare strike a match at the wrong time at night. Could reveal our position to the enemy. Many a gun has been aimed at a match at night. With powerful field glasses, those matches stand out like search lights. A man smoking could cause us to lose several hundred men."

Smoking was a personal habit which Gen. Patton could not stop by giving an order, but he warned the staff about excessive smoking. If any staff officer smoked too much at our officers' mess (meals), this officer would feel Gen. Patton's hand on his shoulder, "Lieutenant, you know you are smoking too much!" Gen. Patton never gave the man a chance to reply. The lieutenant had the message.

After a briefing on lung power and breathing, Gen. Patton would march out of the room or area as straight as an arrow and with his chest as big as a barrel. The men had the message. George Scott had the message when he played the role of Gen. Patton in the movie. He was barrel-chested throughout all of the movie! This lung-oxygen-brain principle was given by Gen. Patton in early 1942, at least thirty years before I remember any doctor prescribing oxygen for patients with failing memories. I have given this deep breathing principle to luncheon clubs and would ask the listeners to try the full lung inflation principle. After one meeting a doctor suggested that this was dangerous for some patients who had never taken a full breath! When I report this suggestion to Gen. Patton in hell or heaven, I am sure he will explode, "Deep breathing dangerous? Do the American people use their lungs so little they cannot breathe?"

I continue to follow this principle especially when I get sleepy on a long drive in a car. One doctor suggested that deep breathing could add ten years to my life.

THERE IS NO POWER
IN A BUSHEL OF BLUBBER

Gen. Patton was not the type of commander who would order men to stand at attention or stand straight to satisfy a whim. His instructions on stature were as humorous as many of his statements. Although the men laughed, they received the instructions.

He would instruct, "A man who cannot see his shoes without bending halfway to the ground has a real problem! He is spending all of his energy driving around a bushel of blubber! Every man needs all of the power he can get. Power comes from that engine in the belly. Great piece of machinery that belly. Put in good food and you get good power back out. If you keep the belly muscles tight you can increase the power of the whole body. I will see that you get the best food I can wrangle out of the quartermasters even if I have to pay for it out of my own pocket. The food you eat turns into power just like gasoline in a car. Your belly should be strong and tight enough to take a dozen saber wounds and never stop going forward. Don't laugh! It can be done! If you can keep going after the enemy has given you several saber jabs, you'll scare the hell out of the enemy!"

The men would laugh but Gen. Patton continued, "It's no big deal to get more power out of the belly. Just pull it in and hold it for ten seconds. Pull it in ten times every time you think of it. That will give you lots of power, and you will be tuned-up like a good engine. A man is a damn fool to die just because he forgot to pull in his bushel of blubber. Every man ought to be able to look down and see his shoes without bending to the ground!"

This principle of strain and pressure was pushed by Gen. Patton long before the term, isometrics, became a household word. Everyone laughed at the General, but his words were not wasted. Every man started pulling in his bushel of blubber for the ten seconds. The troops did increase their power! They did stand straight! They laughed at the idea of taking a dozen saber jabs to scare the enemy, but some of them did go ahead after severe injury. And the enemy was shocked! So shocked that many thousand of the enemy troops surrendered at the sound of Gen. Patton's tanks and soldiers.

KEEP YOUR FEET CLEAN
AND STUDY THE BIBLE

"It's a hell of a lot more important to keep your feet clean than it is to brush your teeth! You do not walk on your teeth! You use your feet all the time to get at the enemy. Keep your feet clean," Gen. Patton preached.

My feet raised Gen. Patton's anger when I had a severe case of athlete's foot. The California desert sand was always hot, and my feet were so infected I limped. When Gen. Patton saw me limping and learned the cause he exploded, "You are too lazy to bend down and scrub your feet! Bend down there and get all of that crud out from between your toes, and you will be able to walk.

As usual, he was right. Now, every time I take a shower or bath I dig out all of the crud as he advised. I have never had a serious foot infection since I followed his advice.

In reading the books about Gen. Patton, I learned that he continued to push for clean feet during the drive through Germany in the middle of the winter. He demanded a new pair of socks for every man every day. He knew the men could not wash their socks.

This "clean feet' principle does not merit any great amount of attention unless you have sore feet. I associate this principle with the washing of the feet in the Bible although Gen. Patton never mentioned this with his foot care briefings. He was always reading the Bible and advised us to do the same. "Read some of the Bible every day! Study those chapters where it talks about the desert of North Africa. We are going to be fighting in that area. You remember every mountain and water hole mentioned in the Bible. It could save your life. The Bible is accurate reporting. If the Bible says there is a source of water the chances are great that it will still be there."

In the Patton movie a newsman asked Gen. Patton if he ever read the Bible which was on Gen. Patton's bedside table. The General responded with profanity that he read the Bible every night. In the movie theater which I attended the audience laughed at how silly it would be for an army general to read the Bible every night. With Gen. Patton, reading the Bible was not a laughing matter.

Gen. Patton **knew** the Bible. He is supposed to have corrected a high ranking church officer on the proper words of a quotation which the church official had used. The church leader reacted with a charge that no man as profane as Gen. Patton should quote any religious verse nor try to correct the clergy.

Gen. Patton reacted with the same degree of anger, stating that the head of such a great church should not utter false religious verses. Gen. Patton, to settle the dispute, ordered an attendant to get a Bible. Before the attendant could return Gen. Patton asked the head of the church for the chapter and verse of the quotation which he had attempted to quote. The church leader could not give either chapter nor verse so Gen. Patton walked to the blackboard and wrote the author, chapter and exact verse. Turning to the audience, he recited the verse. The attendant brought the Bible into the room, and Gen. Patton pointed to the blackboard and ordered the attendant to read the cited verse. As the attendant read, it was obvious that Gen. Patton had quoted the verse correctly, and the head of the church was wrong. The church leader's comment was that he had taken the verse out of context. Gen. Patton smiled and said, "The head of a church should never take the Bible out of context!"

This incident has the sound of a legend, but it was reported as a true story in one of Gen. Patton's biographies. I would hesitate to suggest that it might not be true because the truth about Gen. Patton was usually more amazing than the legends.

KEEP MOVING AND PAIN
WILL NEVER HIT YOU!

It might be difficult to understand how taking a cold shower could be used by General Patton to help men in combat, but Gen. Patton did it! I remember his saying, "Taking a cold shower is just like going into combat. It is only the first second that is hard to take! With a cold shower, if you keep moving around the pain will not hit you in any one spot. When you go into combat, it is the same way. You keep moving and the enemy cannot hit you. When you dig a foxhole, you dig your grave. In a cold shower, keep moving around so the little bullets of cold water will spread the pain all over. Hiding in the corner of the shower is just the same as hiding in a foxhole. You keep moving and jumping and the pain will be so scattered you won't have it! Same way with the enemy. Keep moving forward and you can find out where the bullets are coming from. Then you can kill the bastards. They will be so scared they will surrender before you get there. It is scary when you know someone is coming to kill you no matter what. And that is exactly what we are going to do! We are going to kill the enemy. No matter what."

These words lose some of their power with the elimination of the profanity, but the instructions were taken seriously by the troops. They did take cold showers! When we were in the desert in March of 1942 and using the Colorado river water from the Los Angeles aqueduct, we didn't have any choice. The water was ice cold! I still try to take a cold shower, and I find it will destroy pain. I presume the medical principle is the same as putting ice on pain. The best way to take a cold shower, as General Patton explained, "Is go full-cold all at once! Never inch into a cold shower anymore than you would inch up toward the enemy. Dash into the cold shower! Go into full cold just like diving into a cold swimming pool!"

Gen. Patton also advised taking hot showers for "taking the junk out of the holes in the skin but always finish with cold to close the holes against germs and bugs." Some doctors advise this hot and cold treatment for muscle pain.

Gen. Patton had unusual ideas about body pain. His statements were humorous, "There is nothing new about pain. If you let a little ache or pain drive you to the hospital, you will spend all of your time in bed. More people die in bed than any place else! A lot of pains are from sitting in one place too long. Pain has to be shook loose. The body is a machine. Let it set too long and the mechanical joints get frozen in position. The way to break out of the pain is to get up and go. Remember in the Bible about the sick man who was told by Jesus to pick up his bed and walk. The sick man did get up and walk away. Pain is just like any other enemy. You keep moving around and the enemy cannot hit you. Same way with pain. The quicker you break away from the enemy, the quicker you will drive the pain out of your system. You sit too long and you will not be able to move!"

When the troops laughed, Gen. Patton would smile and finish saying, "I'm damn sure you will move in a cold shower. Keep moving when the enemy starts shootin'."

MAKE THE MIND COMMAND THE BODY
NEVER LET THE BODY COMMAND THE MIND

I remember Gen. Patton saying, "Now if you are going to win any battle you have to do one thing. You have to make the mind run the body. Never let the body tell the mind what to do. The body will always give up. It is always tired morning, noon, and night. But the body is never tired if the mind is not tired! When you were younger the mind could make you dance all night, and the body was never tired. Same way when you went home dead tired from a day of hard work, and some girl would call asking, 'Can you take me to the dance?' Suddenly, the mind assumed command and told the dead-tired body that it was not tired! You had ten times more energy after a day of hard work than you had in the morning! It's the same way in war. When you are tired, the enemy is tireder! You always got to make the mind take over and keep going. Never let the body command the mind. Never let the enemy rest!"

Gen. Patton would ask, "Ever watch a cat stretch out after a long snooze? A cat will stretch every muscle as far as it will go. When did you reach as high as you could reach? When did you put your back and head on the floor and stretch your legs and arms as far as they will go, or try rolling over stretching like a damn cat? Be careful when you do it. Could put you in the hospital for a week!"

Everything Gen. Patton said was geared to combat. I remember one day in the desert he shouted, "Throw away all of your pillows. A pillow is too much to carry around. A pillow is worthless. Keep your head straight and onthe level when you sleep. You will get more oxygen into the brain. Blood will flow on the level better than it will uphill when your head is on a pillow. A damn pillow will reduce your lung power."

So many times Gen. Patton advised, "If you want to have the brains to think tall, you gotta sleep tall, sit tall and stand tall!"

TO GAIN STRENGTH ALWAYS GO
BEYOND EXHAUSTION

Gen. Patton advocated exercise before the medical profession started prescribing physical activity rather than bed rest for many types of medical problems including surgery. He pushed for exercise in 1941, or before the days of getting the patient up the day after surgery. He was preaching exercise before the doctors decided that total bed rest could be final in some types of heart cases.

Gen. Patton would advise, "You got to drive the body to the last inch of energy and then go on. You gain nothing by just going up to where you are exhausted. The body will only build and grow to fit the demands which the mind makes. If all you do is exercise until the body is tired, the body will get lazy and stop a bit shorter every time. You have to go to the point of exhaustion and go on. That way the body will figure out, 'We got to build up more body strength if that crazy mind is going to drive this hard.' If you always quit when you are merely tired, you will not gain. Once you let the body tell the mind when to quit, you are whipped for sure. You cannot gain listening to the body. We can become much stronger. We only use about one-tenth of the available strength of our bodies and less than that of our minds!"

I remembered Gen. Patton's advice when in 1968 one of the top doctors in the space program talked of the problems of exercise for astronauts. This doctor stated that research had indicated that the muscles will not gain in strength by doing something which can be done easily. "To gain strength," the doctor reported, "the body must be exerted to the point of exhaustion and go on." I stopped listening to the space doctor because my mind was racing back to the tall figure of Gen. Patton giving the same advice over twenty-five years earlier.

"Any muscle which is not used will start to decline in strength within a few hours after use," the space doctor added. Gen. Patton would have endorsed this idea. I remember Gen. Patton saying so many times, "We can always take one more step! When we are on the attack we can always go one more mile."

Gen. Patton made these statements in 1942. In the 1978 Yearbook of the Illustrated World Encyclopedia, Laurence Cherry stated, "Doctors often unwittingly play the pain game when they admonish the patient to "take it easy." And so instead of pushing the body a little more each day, the patient exerts his body as little as possible, getting stiffer and his pain becomes more painful." This article was about pain, but the Patton Principle of 1942 was being proclaimed by the medical profession in 1978.

For Gen. Patton it was impossible to go too far. He would say, "We lazy humans only use about half of our total body strength; less than that of our brains. We rust out because we are too lazy to get up a good hot sweat."

For the doctors who advise. "Do not over do." Gen Patton would say, "You damn well better over do or you won't do at all!"

There is truth in both the doctor's and Gen. Patton's advice.

CHAPTER 4

PRINCIPLES OF PRIDE AND CONFIDENCE

PRIDE IN SELF STARTS WITH PRIDE IN APPEARANCE

According to Gen. Patton, to be a soldier was the highest goal man could achieve. No man could walk with as much pride as a soldier who was fighting for his country. Gen. Patton had a clear understanding of fear, faith, and pride. He was constantly striving to kill the fears of every one of his soldiers. Faith and confidence builds pride, and pride destroys fears. No one could build pride in soldiers as quickly as Gen. Patton. The highest tribute any Patton soldier could receive was to be called, "A damn good soldier."

I remember how Gen. Patton instilled pride in every soldier in the Desert Training Center and the I Armored Corps. He did it with his famous neck tie order. The Patton critics who made fun out of this order in their news stories never understood the full impact of the neck tie. I must admit that when I saw the order I was certain that we were in for trouble.

Before relating the story about the neck tie order, a few facts should be stated. I Armored Corps arrived in the California desert without proper uniforms, equipment, tools or supplies. We arrived with almost nothing. Washing our hands, shaving, washing our feet, and bathing was done in the helmet which would hold about two quarts of water.

To know the stature of Gen. Patton, I relate the story of Gen. Patton sending me to Sears in San Bernadino, California. My orders were to purchase all the wash basins which I could find. I remember the shock of the Sears manager when I answered his question of how many wash basins I wanted to purchase.

"A minimum of 100,000!"

The manager exclaimed, "There can't be that many in the whole U.S."

"We will buy all you can locate."

"Who is going to pay for all of these basins?" the manager asked.

"I have authorization from the United States Army and from Gen. Patton on his personal authorization."

"You mean Gen. Patton will pay for this order personally?"

"Yes, you will be paid by either Gen. Patton or the United States Army. You can take your choice."

"I will take Gen. Patton's check. You know he was born around here. There is a town up the road named Patton."

For the next half hour I listened to legends about Gen. Patton.

With the delivery of wash basins to the desert and within thirty days, we had water piped to every camp. We had showers and toilets that flushed. We had everything necessary to keep clean and to keep our uniforms neat. We were wearing the summer tan uniforms which were not cool but much cooler than the winter uniforms some of us had to wear when we first arrived.

I remember the staff meeting which was held about a week before the neck tie order was issued. Gen. Patton outlined what he desired, "We have reached the stage in our training where there is no excuse for any man not to be clean and in proper uniform. All of you old officers that have the faded creamy white uniforms, send those uniforms and get new whites. If you cannot afford new whites, stay away from our dress functions! I want all of my staff tobe in the same color of white! We will not mix our summer tans and dress whites at any function. When we meet with any of the public in the evening we will be in dress whites. When people come out here at any hour of the day, we will be in the summer uniform, shirt during daylight hours and blouse in the evening. Army Regulations will be enforced. No man, officer or enlisted man, leaves this post without being in proper uniform. And that uniform better be clean, and he must be wearing the insignia of the I Armored Corps on his left shoulder. Any man out of uniform or with long hair and dirt, stays on the post. No man can have any pride if he dresses as if he has to go to the bathroom or has just been there."

Gen. Patton did not say anything about neckties, but the necktie was a part of the uniform. There was some complaining from the troops that were turned back from the gate because of their dirty shoes or improper uniform. In some cases, this meant the loss of a two-day pass for Los Angeles. The Military Police would not listen to any excuses because every man had at least thirty days to get his uniform in proper condition.

Gen. Patton knew as we all did that a man could be in proper uniform when he passed the guards at our main gate and sixty seconds later he could have his tie and shirt off. I must admit that I have seen soldiers carrying their shirts and ties as if they were going to the bathroom for a shower.

Gen. Patton attacked this problem with his famous neck tie order. When I saw the order I was sure that we were in for a revolution. I could see hundreds of men being court-martialed for failure to wear the uniform — with the necktie.

When the order was issued I was the General's Judge Advocate or attorney for the command. I could see a need for a dozen typists to type all of the charge sheets!

The Gen. Patton order was simple. It stated that every man leaving the Desert Training Center would be in proper uniform with his neck tie tied and tucked between the second and third buttons of his shirt. Any officer or non-commissioned officer seeing any one out of uniform was ordered to stop the man, get his name, and his organization. If any company commander should have two of his men out of uniform in Los Angeles or Palm Springs, the company commander was ordered to write a detailed letter explaining why two of the commander's men were found out of uniform. This meant that every company commander had to have total control over his men because Los Angeles was over a hundred miles away!

If three men from the same organization were discovered out of uniform, the company commander would be notified and ordered to submit his letter of resignation from the United States Army, or be court-martialed for failure to perform his duties!

I was correct about one thing! There was a revolution over the order but it was not a revolution against Gen. Patton as I had suspected. It was a revolution to be neat, clean and as spit-and-polished as Gen. Patton. Immediately every man was wearing the insignia of the I Armored Corps and having the appearance of being ready for a dress parade. Every man was walking ten feet tall with the pride of belonging to Gen. Patton.

I talked with many of the company commanders to learn how this revolution in appearance had been conducted. I learned that every company commander called his officers together and declared that before he, the company commander, would submit a letter of resignation, every man in the outfit would be "busted" to a buck private. One company commander told me, "I told every one of my men that if they were caught out of uniform, they would be restricted to the desert for the duration!"

If there was any grumbling, it was slight. When a soldier walked a block in Los Angeles or Palm Springs, he could see that his dress was so superior to the average soldier that no soldier would ever think of being anything other than "one of Patton's best." There was a revolution in pride. Pride in appearance was the key which Gen. Patton used to build pride in the hearts and souls of the men.

After the order was issued Gen. Patton made a few remarks which I remember. He said, "As you know I have published an order on neck ties. I want every man to look like a soldier. I will not tolerate any man being half dressed so he looks like he is coming from a bathroom or on his way. He can wait to undress until he gets to the bedroom. He can wait that long! The idea of a soldier looking half-dressed brings disrespect upon the entire United States Army. I do not want any man from our command looking like any other soldier. I want every man to look like he belongs to the I Armored Corps.''

We were still the I Armored Corps although we were also called "The Desert Training Center." The Training Center did not have any insignia. No letters were required. Every commander knew that Gen. Patton would enforce the order. If any should doubt, a form letter of resignation was mailed to every commander. If Gen. Patton demanded a letter of resignation, all that was needed was a signature on the letter.

In enforcing this order, Gen. Patton did what he always instructed us to do. He enforced the existing regulations and did not enact a new. So often some new staff colonel would insist on writing some new regulation for the troops. After limited discussion, Gen. Patton would ask, "Colonel, before we do anything let's see exactly what Army Regulations says. I think we can enforce the old rule and forget about any new regulation." Gen. Patton's memory of Army Regulations was usually correct.

After the neck tie order, Gen. Patton's critics said that he demanded the wearing of the neck tie when on duty in a tank, under a truck and in the field. This was not true. On duty any soldier could wear almost anything which would help him with his work — with one exception. He had to wear the helmet.

Gen. Patton was violent! "I will shoot any man whether he is dead or not if he does not wear his helmet! That helmet can turn away a lot of junk the enemy might send at us. Wear it at all times! We need every man. We cannot lose any man because he is too dumb to wear his helmet. Learn to work in it!''

PRIDE IN SELF STARTS WITH PRIDE IN APPEARANCE

I remember another lecture which Gen. Patton gave the troops about insignia. It was what we called the, "Let-em-know-we-are coming!" lecture. Gen. Patton was soft spoken on this subject. He always started slowly and waited for any laughter. He would say, "Before long we will be going into combat, we can hope! The country needs us to kill those bastards. Combat will be far less exciting than our training here in the desert."

There was laughter. Gen. Patton waited for the laughter before continuing, "When we go into combat I will shoot any man that removes the insignia of our organization or the insignia of his rank. Some generals demand that every man remove all insignia so if captured, the enemy cannot tell what organization they were fighting. We want the enemy to know they are facing the toughest fighting men in the world!"

There was some chuckling and Gen. Patton would order, "We are the best and don't ever forget it!"

Everything was silent as he would state, "For every officer of any rank, non-com or commissioned, I want his rank showing on his helmet. Let that rank be seen! When the officers are leading the men, the enemy knows they are facing a fighting organization and not a group of men being pushed from behind. Any army with the officers in the rear have all of the fighting strength of a bushel of spaghetti being pushed up a hill. Enemy troops will surrender when they see our officers up front!"

There would be some laughter. "Another thing. Don't worry about being captured. You can be sure you will be treated kindly when you are wearing the insignia of our organization. You tell those bastards that if they know what is good for them, they had better surrender because I will never be far away."

There was laughter, but Gen. Patton had made his points. There were thousands of Germans who did surrender when they knew that they were facing Patton's

PRIDE IN SELF STARTS WITH PRIDE IN
APPEARANCE

Third Army. To surrender to Gen. Patton's men was not as great a dishonor as to surrender to any other organization. Many organizations, according to history, would drive into the area of the Third Army so they could surrender with honor!

Habits are not easily broken. It has been over thirty years since I wore a neck tie and tucked the end of the tie between the second and third button of my shirt. Today, quite often I discover that I have left the second button of my shirt unbuttoned. It is then that I remember the neck tie order and think of Gen. Patton as I fasten the second button.

I live in the southwestern part of the United States where casual dress is encouraged because of the heat. I never wear a shirt without a tie without thinking of Gen. Patton. I puzzle over whether this casual dress causes the lack of pride in self, in family, in schools, in churches and country. I admit that in the heat of the summer I wear a shirt outside of my slacks. When I do, I remember Gen. Patton's remark, "Dressed like that a soldier looks like he has just been to the bathroom or has to go!"

NEVER FEAR FAILURE

"All my life I've been shot at! Quite often by the enemy! Only once did the enemy ever hit me with a bullet. Of course, I've had a lot of splatter stuff. No matter what you do, people will be shooting at you. Even your friends. It is true that you have to protect yourself from your friends more than your enemies. The more you do, the more your friends and enemies will say you haven't done. That's the law of life. If you are afraid of being shot at, you are whipped before you start." Gen. Patton gave this briefing to new and old staff members.

I remember Gen. Patton saying that men could be divided into two types, command and staff. We will always need staff officers, and some men will always be staff types. Some men can never be trained to be commanders. He lectured, "We will need good commanders. It is difficult to train good commanders. A man is either a commander or he is not. We must have men who can lead men into battle. In the history of the world there have been few commanders. It takes the right mixture of common horse sense and stupidity to make a commander. Smart men know that any battle plan can fail. If I had any good sense, for example, I would not be in the Army! But damn it, we've got a war to win. If we don't kill the enemy, they will kill us. It takes a lot of courage to lead men into battles where they can be killed. A commander does not dare to have any fears. If a commander shows any fear, the men can tell. When there is fear of failure, there will be failure."

It would be many years before I would grasp the full meaning of Gen. Patton's words. I could not believe that some men refuse to make decisions. These are the staff types. These types can never command. Some men do not want the lead role where all the blame will fall upon them for any failure. I can cite Bing Crosby as an example of a staff type. By Bing's own words on national television, he admitted that he never had a lead role and did not want a lead role in any movie. He said, "If the movie flopped, I would not suffer too great a loss if I could stay away from the lead role." Our society in 1940 did not train commanders. We trained followers, not leaders. We had the gifted child program. We had the honors programs for gifted children who could secure high grades from their teachers. We taught our children that it was terrible not to have high grades. Our children were smarter than their teachers. The children learned that high grades were necessary for admission to college so the students echoed the words of their teachers. They took more courses where it would be easy to get high grades. They exerted effort for high grades and not for knowledge. After a generation of this training, we had a generation of children who had accumulated high grades but could not face the battles of life — the fear of failure and death.

I remember a young man who was a "gifted" child in grade school. In high school he discovered girls, and the high school teachers discovered that his "gifts" were not as high as his grade school grades. When he received his first high school grades, he was average! This could not be tolerated by his parents. Neither he nor his parents could take the failure of being average. The young man was placed in a private school where he would be protected from being average. This young man has never recovered from his fear of being average. He could not take failure! He could not face any enemy. He was not ready for the battle of life and death.

Good commanders must be so stupid that they will attack in the face of fear. Churchill was a fool to say, "We will fight on the beaches, in the streets, in our homes. . . and though this nation last a thousand years, this will be our finest hour!" Not polite words, but he spoke the truth. Any good staff man would have collected all of the facts and said, "We will seek peace in our time." This is an exact quotation from the man who was prime minister of England before Churchill.

NEVER FEAR FAILURE

A good commander is an expert in facing truth.

Gen. Patton charged, "Any man who is afraid of failure will never win! Any man who is afraid to die will never really live!"

NEVER TAKE COUNSEL OF YOUR FEARS

"There is a time to take counsel of your fears, and there is a time to never listen to any fear. It is always important to know what you are doing," Gen Patton admonished.

"The time to take counsel of your fears is before you make an important battle decision. That's the time to listen to every fear you can imagine! When you have collected all of the facts and fears and made your decision, turn-off all of your fears and go ahead!" He continued, "Every plan you make in war is going to be a live-or-die decision. You will either live or die as a result of your decision. Since we are not afraid to do either there is no reason to take counsel of our fears."

He continued, "The chance of being killed in combat is not as great as being killed on our highways. If you want to take counsel of your fears, stop driving a car! And don't crawl in bed at night! More people die in bed than any other place!" We laughed.

When there was time, Gen Patton explained his ideas, saying, "The person who cannot face death has truly never faced life because every day of life is a day closer to death. To take counsel of fears about death is to destroy every day of living."

I had an experience which proved the wisdom of Gen. Patton's principle of never listening to your fears. First, I should relate that my service with Gen. Patton ended in August of 1942. The Army needed pilots, and I was young enough to qualify for the pilot training program. Every pilot was needed because of the high loss-rate of pilots in the bombing missions over Europe. Gen. Patton called me into his office, "Williamson, I cannot hold onto you much longer. The pressure is on to release every man your age for pilot training. I will miss you!"

Months later I was selected to be a Squadron Commander of the first Night Fighter Squadron, flying always at night and in all weather conditions. I am sure I was selected because of my service with Gen. Patton. The task of getting young pilots to fly at night and in all weather conditions was not easy. Every decision was a life and death decision.

Early one morning I was flying a P-70 twin-engine Night Fighter aircraft on a test flight with a rebuilt engine. When only ten feet in the air, the rebuilt engine exploded. There was no time to take counsel of fear. All of the time was spent in trying to get that plane high enough to bail out or to find a suitable place to crash. I finally nursed the plane into the air and back to our own landing field. As I used the good left engine to turn off the landing strip, I called the control tower to ask, "Can you send a tow truck to pull this plane back to the line? I have had some trouble!"

I had previously advised the tower to clear the field of all aircraft for an emergency landing. The tower operator did not need to be told that I was in trouble! He could see the black smoke pouring from the right engine. Following a standard battle plan, I started to write up a bad engine when the tower operator called, "Don't worry if you cannot get out of the plane! The ambulance and fire trucks will be there in a minute!"

I came out of my never listen to fear battle plan and looked at the flames near the gas tank. It was then that I listened to my fears and flipped open the top canopy and jumped off the left wing without a ladder.

In times of danger from fires, floods, combat, cancer, old age, or any serious problem, the mind does not gain by taking counsel of fears. We will get older whether we listen to fears or not. The fear of age can be worse than age. Cancer can cause death from worry as easily as from the disease. If this were not true, so many people would not fear cancer so much that they refuse to have the examination which could result in treatment to destroy cancer.

About a year later, my military service ended with a telephone call from a doctor saying, "We must amputate your leg because of bone cancer."

A few weeks earlier a tumor had been removed from my left knee. Cancer had not been mentioned. I was flying again although with a brace on my left leg. I had returned to San Francisco from an inspection trip in Florida. War does not provide time for proper bedside manners for a doctor. I asked the doctor, "What if I refuse the amputation?"

"You have only about two years to live even with an amputation!" The doctor did not waste words.

There was only one decision. With my fellow officers we made up a slogan, "Don't hesitate! Amputate!"

Gen. Patton's principles helped me through the amputation, and I kept repeating, "Never take counsel of the fears of cancer!" Every day of life was another day. Every day of life pushed death back one day. No one knows how many more days of life remain. If we take counsel of our fears of death, we will never enjoy life.

Ten years later the doctors advised, "You have whipped cancer!" Nine more years and a doctor told me, "Something has to go! You have bone cancer again! We have to take off more of your leg or you will die!" The doctors amputated and left me with only three inches of left leg. They are still three inches from where I live! This second amputation was fifteen years ago. Gen. Patton's principle has helped me through thirty-four years!

There are many examples on the wisdom of refusing to take counsel of fear. An example for me is in walking. With the leg amputations I have been compelled to learn to walk with many different legs. Every fitting of a leg requires learning to walk again. There is a time to be cautious and listen to our fears of falling. However, if when we walk we constantly look at our shoes, we are sure to stumble and fall. Whether we walk with artificial legs or our own legs, we must not look at the ground. Gen. Patton would advise, "Walk tall!" With a wooden leg, if I do not walk tall, the leg does not swing forward properly. When I watch for my left wooden foot come forward, I am sure to fall. The person with good legs who looks at the ground will fall more often than the "walking-tall" person.

Gen. Patton would often give an example to the troops by discussing marriage. It was a humorous lecture. "Fear of combat is just like fear of marriage. When you have dated every girl in the neighborhood, you know enough to either get married or stay single! You have all of the facts. When you have the best training and the best equipment for war, you are ready to kill, and you will not be afraid. There might be a shot fired here and there that might come close, but nothing important to worry about. It is just like marriage; that is, combat and marriage. A stray shot now and then is the same as a fight in a marriage — a little spat could make the marriage better. Combat will make all of us better soldiers!"

There was laughter, but the men learned to silence their fears. Gen. Patton would conclude, "After you make a decision, do it like hell — and never take counsel of your fears over whether you made the right decision or not!"

C H A P T E R 4

PRINCIPLES FOR MAKING DECISIONS

85

WHEN AT WAR WE MUST KILL PEOPLE

Gen. Patton had the ability to get to the bare-boned truth, and he gave the stark truth to the troops. He was blunt, "War means killing people. That's all there is to it. If we are to win we must kill before they kill us."

With this ability to get to the truth and to make the decisions that had to be made, he was far ahead of all of the management experts. His constant command to the staff was, "Get the truth! Get all of the facts! Sound decisions cannot be made without all of the facts."

Gen. Patton in smaller section meetings would comment, "Decision making is an impossible task for some people, and such people should never be in positions of command. Commanders must make decisions, and these decisions are sure to cause men to die. Often the commander making the decisions will cause his own death! This is the reason we do not have many good commanders."

In further explanation of his ideas, Gen. Patton related to flying, saying, "The life of an aircraft pilot depends on his ability to make life and death decisions. At the end of the runway before takeoff, the pilot goes through the check list to make sure the plane will fly. Any mistake in this decision and the penalty is death. At midpoint, roaring down the runway, the pilot must make a second decision: is the plane picking up speed properly or shall the throttle be cut, brakes applied and stay on the ground. The time to make this midpoint decision is less than a tenth of a second. Beyond midpoint on the runway the pilot cannot turn back. In fact, he cannot turn the plane in any direction until safe speed and safe altitude can be secured. Any delay in these decisions and the plane will crash."

In the evening discussions in his tent, Gen. Patton commented, "In life as with flying a plane, some men are never ready to takeoff. Some men want to always stay on the ground, or if they get in the air, they want to turn back when there can be no turning back. Some men cannot make a decision when they know the decision could mean their death."

Gen. Patton used the example of the aircraft because he was a pilot. He had his own small plane which he flew in the desert. He continued to fly his plane until the United States Army could secure a plane for his use! Whenever there was a need, Gen. Patton did not hesistate to spend his own money.

Gen. Patton did not have kind words for those who could not face death. He had harsh words for the religious leaders who opposed the efforts of the military and preached, "Thou shall not kill." Gen. Patton called these types, "pulpit killers!" He commented, "These pulpit killers that go around saying that the Bible says that man dare not kill causes the death of many thousands of good soldiers. Damn little those pulpit killers know about the Bible. They know even less about the way God works. They should read all of the Bible, not just the part they like! God never hesitated to kill. God never hesitates to kill when one man or any race of man needed to be punished. God helped David kill Goliath, didn't he? How about Noah and the Ark? All of the rest of the people were killed in the flood! God took the blame for this mass murder. How about the Red Sea which opened up long enough for one race to escape and another race to be killed. Don't talk to me about God not permitting man to kill. War means that we have to kill people. That's all there is to it. It is a sin not to kill if we are serving on God's side. There is no other way to win. Wars must be won for God's sake. He has a part in every war! The quicker we can kill the enemy, the quicker we can go home and listen to the pulpit killers tell us what we did wrong. If it wasn't for us, those pulpit idiots would be shot for standing in their own pulpits. Our task is to kill the enemy before we are killed."

Gen. Patton was not as harsh with the conscientious objectors as he was with the pulpit killers. He accepted the laws which permitted the COs to refuse to fight where to kill would be necessary. Gen. Patton commented "Not every man can be a soldier. To be a soldier is the highest profession of life. When you find a conscientious objector, get him out of the combat unit as fast as possible. If you do not get him out he will cause many men to die. There dare not be any hesitation when the time comes to pull the trigger to kill. Get the COs and the gold bricks back to civilian life or where they cannot cause the death of our own troops."

Although Gen. Patton was critical of the gold bricks and peace lovers, he did not place all ministers in the "pulpit idiot and killer" class. He invited ministers from the neighboring cities to visit our camp on Sunday to share the church service with the Army Chaplains.

Many accused Gen. Patton of loving war. In fact, the Patton movie script had him saying, "I love war!" Gen. Patton did not love war, but he had the courage to face the truth that all there is to war is killing people. Gen. Patton hated war far more than the "pulpit killers" he condemned. He often quoted the Bible, saying, "There will always be wars and rumors of wars." Gen. Patton hated those military and political leaders who delayed, regrouped, consolidated gains, defended land, dug fox holes, or would permit any act which would prolong the the war without any thought of the soldiers on both sides that would die from the delay.

For some men war was a political game. It was necessary to keep military generals and political leaders happy despite what the cost in the lives of men. An Englishman, Gen. H. Essame, said, "Four times since the break out at Avranches, Patton and his army gave Eisenhower opportunities which might well have proved decisive, shortened the war, saved thousands of lives and left the West in a better strategic posture than it would be more than a quarter of a century later."

It is so easy to think about war as the draft, the training, building planes, moving men and materials, and even of helping the economy. It is so easy to forget that all of the military effort is to kill the enemy.

GRAB 'EM BY THE NOSE AND
KICK 'EM IN THE PANTS

Gen. Patton's basic prinicple was "Grab 'em by the nose and kick 'em in the pants." This is a simple principle, but few management experts or military commanders understand its importance.

Gen. Patton's words were blunt, "We are in war. Wars can be won only by killing people. It is easier to kill people when you can see what you are shooting at. Sure, the planes and guns can drop shells in an area behind the enemy lines. But it does not do much good in killing people. Not many soldiers can be scared to death! We got to go up to the front where we can see the enemy. We'll let the enemy know that we are not afraid. We will let them know that we are coming for only one reason, to kill. If we grab 'em by the nose, they will keep shooting us. But we will keep moving so fast they won't hit us. While we hold their attention they will be shootin' at where we have been, we will get around behind them with our tanks and capture all of their gas, food and supplies. We will kill every one that gets in our way."

Gen. Patton would pause and then add, "We will even capture all of their women!" He talked the language soldiers understood. "We will always keep moving fast. We will never dig foxholes to hide in. When you dig a foxhole, you dig a grave! When you are in that foxhole and fire at the enemy, the enemy knows exactly where you are. Sooner of later he will get you squarely in his sights and you will be dead. You keep movin' and you will never be in the enemy's gun sight."

Gen. Patton would close with his usual words, "Remember, wars are won by killing people. The more we kill, the quicker we will get out of this war. Wars are not won by defending land. Let the enemy have any land he wants if we can get him into a position where we can kill him!"

GRAB'EM BY THE NOSE AND
KICK'EM IN THE PANTS

In World War II many generals tried to fight wars on the principles of defense. Few generals used the principle of speed. Most of the generals used the principles of position. Gen. Patton wanted a position where he could kill the enemy. So many positions were taken with the idea that they could be defended. Gen. Patton did not believe in defense, his theory was that if the enemy was constantly under attack, there would not be any need to defend.

In Viet Nam we never "grabbed the enemy by the nose." We never knew why we were in Viet Nam. Killing people was not the objective. We were not in a war to kill people! I remember hearing a luncheon speaker, a high governmental official, state that a little bit of war in a distant place was good for the economy of the United States.

Fighting a war for the economy would cause Gen. Patton to explode, "Who ever heard of fighting a war to help the economy of the Country? Hell! War is killing people. Trying to say there is such a thing as a little bit of war is like trying to say a woman is a little bit pregnant! Who would have the nerve to tell a soldier that he was dying for stable prices?"

There are many practical applications of the need to grab a problem by the nose and kick it in the pants. The discipline of children requires the prompt action of facing the enemy, the child that needs discipline.

Too often a mother will say, "You disobeyed again! Wait until your father gets home. He will punish you." When the tired father comes home, he may say, "Why can't we wait until morning? We might keep our child from sleeping. Let's wait until he does it again!"

Too often the delay gives the child the chance to take all of the "attack" positions so that he can demand the surrender of his parents. The child that is grabbed by the nose and spanked in the pants will appreciate that the parents are teaching the child how to make the mind control the body.

GRAB'EM BY THE NOSE AND
KICK'EM IN THE PANTS

The fears of retirement and death can use this principle.
So often retirement hits like a surprise attack from an
enemy. Few attempts are made to grab retirement by the
nose and kick it in the pants. Many of us do not catch the
principle that every day of life is one day closer to
retirement; also, a day of life is one day closer to death,
Failure to grab death by the nose causes us to live our last
few years in a constant state of fear. When the life ex-
pectancy is down to a few years, the enemy (death) may
be in total command. If death is not grabbed by the nose,
we could be in a "foxhole" of depression from which we
cannot escape.

Gen. Patton's principle is simple to state but difficult to
apply. Many organizations never actually grab the enemy
(problem) by the nose. Many governmental agencies
never grab their mission by the nose and solve the
problem.

I am not sure that Churchill ever caught the importance
of speed in winning wars. Churchill's physician did not
understand the importance of Gen. Patton's principles
when he wrote in his book, "Patton was an unusual
general; he was not much good at fighting a battle, but he
was the best pursuit general of recent years. If Monty
(Montgomery) had been as good in pursuit as he was in
fighting a battle, then he would have been one of the great
captains."

Gen. Patton would never fight a battle as Churchill and
Montgomery fought battles. Gen. Patton would say, "It's a
waste of fine young men to stay in fixed positions and see
who can send over the most shells It costs too many men
to stay in fixed positions where the enemy can strike.
We will keep moving and the enemy will always hit where
we have been and not where we are. When the enemy is
firing at where we have been, we can tell exactly where
they have their firepower. We will move fast and destroy
the enemy where he can be easily killed."

GRAB'EM BY THE NOSE AND
KICK 'EM IN THE PANTS

"Never let the enemy pick the battle site. We will fight where we want to fight and not where the enemy wants to fight. We will always keep the odds on our side." This principle is discussed in the chapter on the rules for winning. Gen. Patton would never fight the day-in-day-out battle of sending shells at locations. Gen. Patton did not want to destroy a bridge or location which might have to be reconstructed for a fast advance. Montgomery was always regrouping, consolidating gains, and waiting for reinforcements! All of this caused Gen. Patton to announce, "To hell with regrouping. We will regroup on the run. Let the women and children consolidate our gains. When we get the enemy on the run, we will keep him on the run."

Many military and management leaders fight their battles on the principles of maintaining positions. Few understand Gen. Patton's principle of "Grab the enemy by the nose and kick them in the pants." Few of us face the truth that every day of life is one day closer to death.

MAN IS THE ONLY WAR MACHINE

Gen. Patton constantly stressed that "man is the only war machine." In his lectures and in the staff meetings he would say, "All of this talk about super-weapons and push button warfare is a pile of junk. Man is the only war machine. Man has to drive the tanks, fly the planes, crawl through the mud, pull the triggers, and push the buttons. We must train to be strong in body and mind. Always remember man is the only war machine."

No general I ever knew had such a clear picture of war and the necessity of training for war. We smiled at his simple ideas, but his ideas were sound.

"It is nice to have good equipment," he would lecture. "A tank is a great weapon for killing. So is the machine gun. But man is the key. Remember the French Revolution? That battle was won with brooms, sticks and stones—by a bunch of angry women. Get a determined bunch of men and women, and they will win the battle no matter what the odds nor what kind of equipment they have. We won the Revolutionary War, didn't we? It was against a far superior military force. Remember what they used in the first battle? They cut logs and rolled them down the hill at the enemy. Rolling logs did not kill, but it sure scattered the troops so they could not fire their muskets."

Now and then some exhausted officer would fall asleep during the long Gen. Patton lectures. Gen. Patton would go to the officer and tap him on the shoulder, "How long you been without sleep?"

If the officer reported anything less than forty-eight hours, Gen. Patton would go into a rage about staying awake for at least forty-eight hours when in combat. If the man had a valid excuse for sleeping, Gen. Patton would order him out of the room to get sleep.

"You give me ten good men unafraid to die, and I can destroy an enemy division of ten thousand. That is, if the ten men will stay awake!" Gen. Patton smiled.

One of Gen. Patton's greatest talents was the ability to eliminate fear in the minds of the men. He eliminated the fear in his own mind and gave the same ability to the troops. He considered fear to be the first enemy to be destroyed. "Face a fear and it will disappear" was one of his principles.

His most famous anti-fear speech was called the "blood and guts" lecture. Within hours after new troops were under the command of Gen. Patton they would get the blood and guts speech. This speech would be given to large numbers of troops near a hill in the desert. Gen. Patton would stand on the highest point with only a pipe-stand microphone. He stood straighter than the iron pipe holding the mike. Staff officers were supposed to attend every lecture so they could get the reaction of the troops. I regret that I have not been able to find a tape of any of these sermons nor a copy of the actual text. I heard the sermon so many times, I can report it from memory without missing many words except for the profanity.

Gen. Patton would lecture, "Men! Don't worry about being scared! Every man is scared when he goes into combat. Any man who says he isn't is a damn liar. I know! I've been in combat, and I've been scared. There is something wrong with a man who isn't scared. Now, I can tell you when you will stop being scared. When that first shell hits and you take your hand, wipe your forehead, and find the blood and guts of your best friend on your hand— you will stop being scared. You will know exactly what to do! You will kill those bastards that killed your friend before they kill you. That is war! You either kill or get killed. Don't worry about being scared, you will know what to do!"

We called this lecture the "gory sermon", but the blood and guts frankness gave the troops a true understanding of war. The troops gained the courage to be able to overcome their fears. If Gen. Patton was willing to admit being scared, they could be scared.

Newsmen called Gen. Patton "Old Blood and Guts" and wrote, "It is the blood of the troops given for Patton's guts." We did call him, "Blood and Guts," at times, but it was for the lecture and not for ordering troops into foolish battles. On any battlefront at any time, Gen. Patton could and would appear to be with the troops in the thick of the enemy fire. He faced the same fears that the men faced.

After destroying the fears of the men, Gen. Patton used every trick in the book to build confidence. The pearl handled pistols (we always called them pearl and not ivory) were symbols to destroy fear and build confidence in the minds of the soldiers. I remember the first day he wore the pistols because I had a camera and took his picture. These pistols were loaded and strapped on Gen. Patton's hips in January 1942. We received a few rounds of 45 cal. ammunition for our automatic pistols so we were on the small arms firing range at Fort Benning, Georgia. The only equipment I had was an empty pistol holster and a camera. Higher ranking officers had the pistols and fired at the targets before the lieutenants could fire. In January we had targets with large circles with the small black center. These targets were soon changed to the shape of a man in the uniform of the enemy. In January of 1942 we had a dozen staff officers and half a dozen pistols.

When Gen. Patton was talking to Col. Gay, I snapped their pictures.

Col. Gay asked, "General, where did you get those fancy pistols?"

note -- The picture of Gen. Patton, Col. Gay and the pistols was sent to the West Point Academy for the Patton Museum. This museum was subsequently established at Fort Knox, Kentucky. The picture has not been lost but is unavailable for this printing.

"I shot a Mexican general out of his saddle when I was with Gen. Pershing in Mexico. Now ask me what I am going to do with them?"

"What are you going to do with them?"

"I am going to shoot that SOB Rommel and throw these pistols in his face!"

The story of the pistols and the Mexican general has been told many times. I did not believe the story about the saddle shoot-out. In fact, I never made any study of Gen. Patton's World War I experiences until after World War II. Several years after World War II, I was introduced to a retired officer who had been the driver of the automobile from which Gen. Patton had fired at the Mexican general. The driver related the story, "We were driving past what looked like an old deserted farm house. It was a rough road for an automobile. This man rode from behind the house and started shooting at us. Gen. Patton shouted, 'Stop this car!' I stopped but before I could get the car stopped, Gen. Patton was on the running board and fired across the top. His first shot killed the man. We could see then that it was a general."

These pistols created more international confidence than Churchill's two-finger salute of "V" for Victory. Churchill's confidence "V" lost meaning within a few months after it was first used. The public did not want to think about the harsh facts of war. Churchill's "V" was used at the time the invasion of England was certain. Churchill used the "V" about the time he made the famous speech, "When this nation is invaded we will fight on the beaches, we will fight in the streets, we will fight in our homes...and although this nation may last a thousand years, this will be our finest hour." But the two-finger "V" did not mean victory, It meant death! It meant take one with you! Churchill used simple math to prove that

England could win. There were more Englishmen than Germans. When the invasion of England came, Germany could not win if every Englishman would kill one German before the Englishman died.

Within a few months, the English used the "V" for victory and forgot that the price of victory could mean death. Gen. Patton would never let any soldier forget that the price of winning any war is to kill the enemy. He used every method to build confidence in the men to kill. During the day he drove in an open jeep among the troops as he advanced towards the front. Gen. Patton never wanted the soldiers to see him returning to his headquarters. Gen. Patton wanted the troops to see him going forward towards the enemy. As Gen. Patton moved forward during the day with the troops, his staff made plans for a small plane to land on a road or field near the front. After dark or at dusk, Gen. Patton would meet the pilot of this small plane and return to his headquarters by air so that the troops would never see Gen. Patton "retreating!"

IN THE LONG RUN, IT IS WHAT WE DO NOT SAY THAT WILL DESTROY US

I doubt that Gen. Patton was the first to state that failure to speak could cause total destruction, but he followed the principle more than any other leader. He spoke the truth when the leaders of the public did not want the truth spoken. He violated all of the rules in current usage, such as "Don't make waves," "Don't fight city hall," Keep your mouth shut and you will never get into trouble," Never speak if it will create ill will," "Right or wrong -- stick with the establishment," and "Don't say anything if it might irritate an enemy!"

I never remember Gen. Patton speaking from prepared speech notes. I remember that he seldom used a speaker's lecturn or table to hold speech notes. When he spoke to the troops in the desert, all that he used was a floor or hand microphone. He did not use notes. I remember helping to write speeches for some of the higher ranking colonels, but never for Gen. Patton. He did not have a prepared speech, and everything he said was his own thinking.

Gen. Patton's attacks upon false ideals hiding the truth caused all of us to worry when he spoke in public. He never hesitated to grab a problem by the nose and shake out the truth. I remember him saying, "This war was caused by every last one of us. No one spoke out against Hitler. Everybody wanted peace in his own lifetime. If any leader of any country had spoken out against Hitler, we would not be fighting this damn war. Only Churchill spoke out against Hitler, but Churchill's power did not come in time to prevent this war. It is what we did not say that caused this war. In trying to buy peace in our life time, we will have to pay the price of losing thousands of our finest young men."

I remember at staff meetings some senior colonel would suggest that Gen. Patton tone down his remarks about our war policies. He refused. He constantly gave the exact truth to the troops and to the press.

I remember a colonel who was trying to be helpful and

IN THE LONG RUN, IT IS WHAT WE DO NOT SAY THAT WILL DESTROY US.

suggested that there was some merit in the motto, "See no evil, hear no evil, and speak no evil."

Gen. Patton went into one of his impromptu briefings saying, "Evil must be destroyed whenever it appears. You hear your kind of garbage every day, but let me tell you something, it is foolish to say that you should never get into a professional contest with a skunk. Let me tell you something! If you don't kill the first skunk that shows up, he will get under the house and you will have to burn the house down to get rid of the devils." These words are not exactly what Gen. Patton said. He used profanity, with his message!

There was laughter and when the laughter stopped, Gen. Patton continued, "Look at Pearl Harbor! No one wanted to get into this war. Any fool could see it coming. We let the skunks get under our front porch, and so we had to burn at Pearl Harbor."

Gen. Patton was considered a rash outspoken reckless military type who wanted nothing but war, but war was what Gen. Patton would try to prevent. If if was necessary to get into war, he wanted to get in and get out as quickly as possible -- with victory. I remembered Gen. Patton's words about the power of silence to destroy when the Watergate explosion hit the newspapers. In addition to all those who were directly involved and went to jail, how many hundred had knowledge of the illegal acts and said nothing. How easily Watergate could have been avoided if the skunks had been stopped before they dug under the front porch.

As history is being written, Gen. Patton's principles are proving correct. The respect for Gen. Patton is growing and gaining throughout the world. Many of the military leaders of World War II who opposed Gen. Patton have been forgotten or have lost respect. The establishment leaders will be lost from memory because of their failure to speak when the truth should have been spoken.

The stories of Gen. Patton talking with the troops are numerous. Many of these stories are true; many are legends. The most amazing stories are usually true. I remember an incident in the Desert Training Center on a hot afternoon. Gen. Patton spotted a man on a telephone pole near our camp. The man was not in proper uniform for the desert. This man was wearing a large flat plantation owner type of hat. We were supposed to wear the fiber helmets. Gen. Patton ordered the man to climb down. The man gave some short greeting and continued to work. Again Gen. Patton ordered him to climb down. The man continued to splice wires and did not answer Gen. Patton.

Gen. Patton shouted, "Come down from that pole! I am Gen. Patton, and I am ordering you down."

"I don't know anything about your problem or who you are, but I cannot take time to come down. I got work to do."

"You come down or I will shoot you down. You have disobeyed an order, and as your superior officer I have the right to shoot you down."

"If you shoot me off this pole you'll go to jail for murder. The only man who can order me off this pole is my telephone supervisor. He would shoot me if I didn't stay on this job!"

"You with the telephone company?" Gen. Patton asked.

"Right! We got some mad general coming in here with a big army. They want hundreds of telephone lines. I wish you would go on about your business so I can finish this splice."

Gen. Patton smiled, "Continue with your work. I thought you were a soldier under my command. That tan shirt and matching pants fooled me. Get that splice finished. I am the mad general your supervisor wants to avoid!"

One morning I was riding with Gen. Patton in the desert. We were about thirty miles from base camp. Gen. Patton was surveying the area with his field glasses watching the movement of the tanks and supporting equipment. He spotted a truck on the paved highway several miles away. During the desert maneuvers no army vehicle was permitted on the highway. Every vehicle had to move on the desert sand. Although it was over ten miles to the highway, Gen. Patton ordered the driver to chase the slow moving truck. When we caught the truck, Gen. Patton waved the driver to the side of the highway.

"What's the problem, soldier? Can't you take the desert? You know that no army vehicle is permitted on the highway during maneuvers." Gen. Patton was ready to attack.

"General, I can take the desert, but this truck can't! I am trying to save the transmission by limping back to base camp. You ask me what's the problem? I'll tell you. You keep asking for more men and equipment to get into the desert. My commanding officer keeps trying to keep you happy. Well, if we lose many more trucks we won't have enough equipment to haul our rations back from Indio, and we will have to haul them in a handbasket!"

"You still having trouble getting parts?" Gen. Patton asked.

"Same as always. We can't keep trucks repaired without repair parts."

"What seems to be the problem with the transmission?"

"General, they just don't make the transmission for this desert heat. Somehow they gotta put a cooler on that oil or we will not be able to move.

Gen. Patton asked to be shown the trouble spot. Both Gen. Patton and the army sergeant were on their knees looking under the truck. The sergeant pointed to the leaking transmission fluid.

Before we left, Gen. Patton gave the sergeant a drink from his canteen and congratulated the soldier for caring for his army truck more than he did for obeying his commanding officer. Gen. Patton asked the sergeant to write a report on the heat problem. While we were still in voice range, Gen. Patton said, "That sergeant is a damn good soldier." The sergeant beamed with pride. Gen. Patton ordered me to follow the transmission problem with copies of the report to Washington and to the truck manufacturer.

Women were not spared from Gen. Patton's wrath although they were not in the Army. Gen. Patton saw a car with a flat tire. We were on the main highway returning to base camp after several days in the desert. The car with the flat tire had a Georgia license plate. A soldier in uniform was helping the woman with the tire. The woman was in extremely short shorts, and women did not wear such short shorts in 1942. Gen. Patton immediately assumed that the woman was what he termed a "camp follower." Gen. Patton stopped, determined to get the soldier on his proper duty.

"Soldier, why are you leaving your duty assignment to help this camp follower?" Gen. Patton demanded.

"I will not be on any duty assignment for three more days, and this woman is not a camp follower. She is my wife!"

Gen. Patton apologized, and we stayed with the couple until they were driving on the highway. In staff meetings, Gen. Patton would instruct, "Always talk with the troops! They know more about the war than anybody. Make them tell you all of their gripes. Make sure they know we are doing everything we can to help them. The soldiers have to win the war. We cannot do it. Talk with them. They will not trust you if you do not trust them."

Gen. Patton walked back and forth in silence. He knew that his little silent walks in front of the staff had a great impact. He finished saying, "Always remember in talking with the troops the most important thing to do is listen!"

Gen. Patton was concerned about every man of every rank. He talked with all of the soldiers. He touched the soldiers with a hand shake or a slap on the back. No man was so dirty or greasy that Gen. Patton would decline to shake his hand. The military hand salute was to be given by the troops to the officers. Gen. Patton did not hesitate to salute the soldiers before they saluted him. If a man deserved a compliment, Gen. Patton would snap to attention and salute the man for his work. When we were in the dust and dirt of the desert and the salute was not required, I have seen soldiers try to form a straight line and salute Gen. Patton when he would drive past their area.

Gen. Patton did not require the troops to do foolish formations or hold vain parades. I do not remember of any parade which Gen. Patton required of the troops. There was a time when a parade had some training value but not with tank warfare. Every meeting of a large number of soldiers was with Gen. Patton on parade. He would stand in front of the men and talk with them about the objectives of the training programs.

I remember a colonel wanting to start a rifle drill team with competition among all of the units for the best drill team. Gen. Patton denied the request, saying, "Drill teams are for peace time armies when the troops have little to do. We have a war to win. I do not want any man using a rifle as a toy. I want every man using that rifle with intent to kill!"

NO ONE IS THINKING IF EVERYONE
IS THINKING ALIKE

It was not necessary for staff officers to agree with Gen. Patton. He followed Ben Franklin's idea of no one was thinking if everyone was thinking alike. Gen. Patton did not want staff officers that would follow his every whim. He was harsh with officers who would differ and not give valid reasons for the difference of opinions.

I remember an arrogant newly commissioned National Guard colonel who objected to a training plan which our staff had prepared.

Gen. Patton said to the colonel, "Give your reasons for objecting to this training plan."

"It just won't work."

"Why?" The new colonel had not learned that when Gen. Patton started using the simple question, "why?" a storm was brewing.

"The plan is too ambitious with too little time." The colonel was not losing his arrogance.

"Why?" Gen. Patton asked. "Give us reasons. This command will not play hunches. War is too dangerous to play hunches. A lot of men can get killed when we do not base our battle plans on facts. What are your reasons for objecting to this plan, colonel?"

"I just don't think it will work!"

Gen. Patton went into a temper display. "Now there is your problem, colonel! You just don't think! I will not have any non-thinkers on this staff. Wars are not won by non-thinkers."

The colonel was silent. The arrogance was gone.

Gen. Patton continued, "We have to be thinking every second. That is the reason for the deep breathing. We got to get oxygen to the brain. Battle plans must be based on facts — cold hard solid facts. If we do not get the facts, we cannot make good decisions. We will lose battles and men will be killed that should live. Every officer and every man must think for himself and be thinking every second. I want my orders followed after we decide on a battle plan,

but I will not have any men around who "just don't think."
We may have different ideas, but we will settle on one
battle plan and that will be the plan we will use. Not
because it is mine but because it is the best plan based on
cold hard facts. That's the whole idea of these staff
meetings. When we decide on the best plan, every man will
know it is the best plan - and he will know why it is the
best."

Gen. Patton hesitated, "There is no place for any man in
any war who does not think. Do you have any questions
about this plan, colonel?"

"No, sir!" the colonel replied.

"Is there anything you want to say about this plan?"

"No, sir," the colonel answered without any arrogance.

This colonel never attended another staff meeting. It
was easy to differ with Gen. Patton, but there had to be
valid reasons. I remember one staff meeting when I was
on the spot for a decision which I had made when I was
Judge Advocate. I decided to court-martial one of our
regular army majors who had been involved in an auto
accident on the road between Indio and Palm Springs,
California. The cause of the accident was drunken driving
on the part of the major.

At the scene of the accident, the major had been abusive
and profane to the ladies in the car which the major had
hit. In addition, the major had insulted the arresting officers of California. These state officers took all of the
major's abuse and returned him to our military police in
the Desert Training Center although they had the legal
right to put him in jail in Indio or Palm Springs.

On the following Monday morning, the major was sober
and on duty with his troops. When the facts were given to
me by the Military Police, I advised that the major had to
be court-martialed for his criminal act of driving a car
while under the influence of liquor. This decision could
result in a fine of several hundred dollars, a sentence in
jail, and could include dismissal from the service.

NO ONE IS THINKING IF EVERYONE
IS THINKING ALIKE

I discussed my decision with our Chief of Staff. The charges were filed and the major was arrested. The charges were forwarded to our higher headquarters for approval and for the calling of a general court-martial, the highest military court.

The controversy started immediately, and there were many arguments for the major. It was only a few months after Pearl Harbor. We were in war. We needed every military officer we could get. The major was a West Point graduate and a trained officer. It was not a crime for a soldier to drink. I was under personal attack. The rank of Judge Advocate was supposed to be a full colonel. I was only a lieutenant. I was too young and had been given too much authority.

All of these arguments reached a climax when the court-martial papers were returned with the instructions that the major be reprimanded, given a pay deduction, and returned to duty with the troops.

Gen. Patton reviewed the case at a staff meeting since it was the subject of daily discussions among the staff and the troops. I remember his closing words, "Lieutenant, your decision has put us in an embarrassing position with our higher headquarters. What is the explanation for your decision?"

I started to answer from the back of the room. Gen. Patton stopped me, saying, "Get on up here, Lieutenant, so you can be seen and heard."

I walked to the front of the room and faced the high ranking officers. They were wearing their war faces. I hope I started slowly, "I agree with all that has been said about the major being a good officer. He is known to all of us. The truth is he did have an auto accident. The truth is that he was so drunk he could not stand up for the California law enforcement officers when asked to walk the center line of the highway. The major couldn't take one step. The truth is these officers returned him seventy miles to base camp. The major was delivered over to our Military Police because we promised the California officers that we would prosecute the major for his driving while under the influence of liquor."

I could sense that I was not gaining so I decided to answer Gen. Patton's direct question. "To answer the question about embarrassing our Command. It should never be embarrassing to follow our own military laws and the laws of the State of California. We should not be embarrassed by following the promise which our Military Police made to the California officers. If our MP's had not agreed to prosecute this major, he would be in jail in Indio under indictment by the laws of California. We have some obligation to the law enforcement officers of California."

I suspected that I might be gaining a few supporters. I attacked all of the staff with the questions, "Is there any man who could expect to swear at and insult women and not expect to be court-martialed for conduct unbecoming an officer and a gentleman? Is there any of you that would get drunk, have an auto accident, and expect to receive only a reprimand for swearing at local police? If any of you would answer affirmatively, what kind of an example do you think it would be for the men you command? What kind of an embarrassing position would you be in with the State of California?"

I looked at Gen. Patton who was standing by a window at the side of the briefing room. His expression did not change as I looked at him for support. I decided to close with some of Gen. Patton's own words, " Gen. Patton has said so many times that we are in war. We try to make our conditions in the desert as close to combat conditions as possible. Any officer who cannot control his drinking in California could not control his conduct in combat. Gentlemen, I want to answer some of the personal attacks which have been made on me."

NO ONE IS THINKING IF EVERYONE
IS THINKING ALIKE

I expected Gen. Patton to stop me, but he did not change position nor expression at the window.

"I am not on trial in this case as it might appear. I could be on trial if I had failed to do my duty as the Staff Judge Advocate as any of you would be on trial if you failed to perform your duty. To answer your charges that I have been too hard on the major, there is evidence that the major released military secrets in Palm Springs. He told the people in one of the bars the exact number of men in the desert, the amount of the payroll and the exact hour and date the money leaves Indio to pay all of the men in this command. I filed only one charge, but I could have filed many. I know that I am young and that I am the only attorney on the staff at this moment. It is not a pleasant task to file criminal charges against a fellow officer. But if we are embarrassed, how embarrassed would this command be if I had not filed these charges?"

I looked at Gen. Patton indicating that I was finished. I remained in front of the staff.

From the window, Gen. Patton asked, "Any of you want to ask Lieutenant Williamson any questions?"

No one said a word. I returned to the back of the room.

Finally, Gen. Patton spoke, "Lieutenant, you are right and our higher headquarters is wrong. You write a nasty reply to our higher headquarters. Just tell them exactly what we are going to do. Get it out today. I will sign it and get it on its way."

The major was transferred with the court-martial charges following him. I never heard what happened in the trial.

KNOW WHAT YOU KNOW AND KNOW
WHAT YOU DO NOT KNOW

"How do we know that?" Was a frequent question of Gen. Patton's at staff meetings.

Some new member of the staff might say, "The information came from Washington."

"That is the most unreliable source of information you could ever get!" Gen. Patton would explain, "An officer in a swivel chair in the Pentagon actually knows little or nothing. All that he knows he gets from the soldiers in the field. I do not want to come down too hard on these men in the Pentagon, but they know almost nothing from first hand knowledge. They merely collect paper facts from the field organizations."

Gen. Patton would continue, "We must always know exactly what we know and what we do not know - and never get the two confused. We can cause many men to lose their lives if we get confused. That is the fault of having our Army controlled from Washington. The officers in the Pentagon seldom get in the field to know what is going on."

Gen. Patton would instruct us to sort through our known and unknown facts to determine exactly what we knew. It could be a shipment of new tanks from Detroit. Some officer might state that the tanks were shipped on a certain date because the shipping notice stated that they were shipped on that date. Gen. Patton would explain, "That is merely the paper work! The man in the office typing up shipping notices probably did not know that the tanks were on the flat car and shipped. The tanks could be on the flat car and still be in the railroad yard because the train has not hooked onto the tanks to get them going."

From the various bits of information we would sift through all of the paper facts about the tanks and determine exactly what we knew. Upon this knowledge we based our plans for the use of the tanks in our desert area. Gen. Patton would finish, "I want one man to follow-up on these tanks. Stay with them every day and with the paper work. Know where those tanks are constantly. If they get side-tracked in some railroad yard, raise hell!"

KNOW WHAT YOU KNOW AND KNOW
WHAT YOU DO NOT KNOW

This type of efficient management saved thousands of hours in staff meetings. No time was wasted on what we did not know. Every officer from the newest second lieutenant to the highest general would not waste time on paper facts. We did not lose much time with the Tech Manuals which were sent to us from Washington to help us plan our troop and tank movements.

Gen. Patton would lecture, "Every tank is different, just like people. Make sure every driver knows his tank and knows exactly how many gallons of gas and oil that tank will use per mile and per hour at different speeds and conditions. Do not rely on the general information from Washington. Check the tank every time it is refueled. If it is taking a lot of oil, send it to the shops. We must **know** our equipment."

Gen. Patton would defend the Pentagon as often as he attacked, saying, "Now where would an arm chair officer get his facts on the gas use of a tank in the field? From the company that manufactured the tank! Now what will the manufacturer say about his tanks? He is sure to cut the gas to the bare minimum to make his tank look good. The manufacturer sends this information to a supply sergeant in Washington who adds all of this into a table, adding 20 percent more to be sure. This goes to a lieutenant who adds a bit more just to be sure he is not wrong. Keep passing these paper facts up the ladder of command and you could have twice as much gas as needed. This type of confusion can work both ways if there is some reason to try to cut the costs or decrease the requirements."

Gen. Patton would continue, "Wars are won by knowing exactly what we know. We must know our needs. If we try to carry into combat more gas, oil and supply parts than we need, it could be as destructive as trying to have a soldier carry a field pack weighing ten more pounds more than he needs. We must cut to the bone, know what we need and what we do not need."

One day our gas supplies were low for all of the Desert Training Command. We planned a one day maneuver. One lieutenant filled all of his tanks to the top. When he was questioned about using so much gas, he answered, "The Tech Manual says that the gas tanks must be filled to the top at all times to prevent moisture accumulating in the tank and causing rust!"

When Gen. Patton learned that one unit of tanks was missing because of lack of gas, there was an explosion. Gen. Patton scolded, "Not one damn gas tank will ever rust out before this war is over! How much moisture is there in the desert? Forget about rust in the tanks! We will move so fast rust will never catch us. Know exactly what every tank needs for the maneuver. Ration it with a definite reserve, but don't always fill 'er up as if you were pulling into a service station. We are trying to learn how to run these tanks to kill enemy soldiers. We are not in this war to prevent rust in the gas tanks!"

In a sober lecture, Gen. Patton would explain, "Every driver must know his tank and what he needs to run that tank. He dare not be worried about whether he has too little gas. He must know. When he knows he will stop worrying."

When there was time, Gen. Patton would give his boyish grin and say, "Relax a few minutes. and I will tell you how to lose wars. Wars are won by the little things, often at unimportant cross roads. In the Louisiana maneuvers last year, 1941, we had a Chinese national enlisted in our American Army. He looked like any other American soldier in his uniform except that he did not understand much English and spoke almost no English. Well, this poor soldier got lost on one of the maneuvers. Being unable to speak English he could not ask where his outfit was located. I doubt that he could pronounce the name of his outfit so any American could understand him. Being in the American uniform and walking along the highway, civilian drivers would give him a ride until the Chinese soldier would open the car door indicating he wanted out. This poor soldier at last was stranded at a cross road where he attempted to hitch hike a ride with any Army vehicle of any unit. The problem was he used his index finger to hitch instead of his thumb. He pointed forward with his finger instead of thumbing backward with his thumb. You can guess what happened. For one Army convoy, the Chinese soldier pointed his index finger down one road. Of course, no vehicle would stop since they knew he was directing traffic. When the trucks failed to stop, he moved to another road and with the next convoy pointed down the new road. All of one entire afternoon, this soldier split our Army units by sending them down first one road and then another."

Gen. Patton paused, "Do all of you realize how easy it would be for one enemy soldier in an American uniform to destroy our firing capability? Well, this story does not get any better. Half a dozen officers stopped and tried to tell this Chinese soldier how to direct traffic. When they discovered that he could not speak English, they gave up in disgust. These officers did not know enough to know that this soldier was not directing traffic. The Chinese soldier knew more than the officers. He was lost and he knew it! Well, that Chinese soldier deserves a medal for teaching us how to lose wars. Always know where your outfit is going. If you do not know, admit it and find out. Would you believe it took us over a week to locate all of the troops this Chinese soldier sent in the wrong directions. We scattered troops, trucks and tanks all over Louisiana and Texas!"

Several times Gen. Patton mentioned this Chinese soldier in the evening meetings in his tent. I was fortunate enough to be included. I remember him saying, "So many people in this world are as confused as our Chinese hitch-hiker who pointed with his index finger instead of his thumb? How many cannot put into words exactly what they know and what they want out of life. We get a ride here and take a trip there, but we never really **know** where we are going. We live our lives like the Chinese hitchhiker.''

Several weeks after Gen. Patton told the story we were in his tent with one of our highest ranking colonels who confessed, "General, your pearls of wisdom hit me harder than all of the rest. I am the SOB that gave that Chinese soldier his military police armband so the troops would know what he was doing! I have never had the guts to admit it. I tried to talk to this man and all he would say was "No-eat, no-eat!" I would point northeast. So he would point northeast with the next convoy! We sent some troops back to the point where they came from! It was long after this whole thing happened that it came to me that this soldier was not saying "northeast" but was trying to say he was hungry!"

We laughed. Gen. Patton said, "I should keep you from getting your general's star!"

The colonel replied, "You would have every right to block my promotion! But I can tell you this. In training or combat, I am going to check every MP at every crossroad. Better we should hold the convoys in position than scatter troops all over the countryside."

This colonel finished the war with four stars. Gen. Patton did not stop his promotion.

GET UP FRONT

One of Gen. Patton's frequent statements was "Get up front!" The civilian rule would be "Get on site." His words aroused laughter. He would say, "I want every officer up front at least once a day. You will never know what is going on unless you can hear the bullets. You must lead the men. It is easier to lead than to push." He would remain silent for several minutes and then continue, "Besides, having the senior colonels up front is a great incentive and temptation for the younger officers. Nothing like a vacancy to help get a promotion!"

He would give his wide grin, and we would laugh. His point had been made. Every officer had to be such a leader of his men that he would not dare show any fear of the enemy nor fear of being shot by his own men. The non-leader would never take a chance of getting in front of his men. Hatred for poor officers could exceed the hatred for the enemy. Gen. Patton insisted on the type of leadership where no senior officer would fear being shot by his own troops.

Some have said that Gen. Patton was hated by his troops. This is a total untruth. Gen. Patton was near the front often enough that many of his men could have used a stray bullet to express their hatred. No one ever tried. My suspicion is that many German soldiers had chances to shoot Gen. Patton. I am sure that many German soldiers saw his shining helmet on the front line. Gen. Patton's leadership was so intense that any German soldier with an ounce of knowledge would have been afraid to kill Gen. Patton. The Germans knew that with Gen. Patton killed, the American troops would be so enraged that no German prisoners would be taken alive for weeks. The Germans knew that when they faced Gen. Patton's troops there was a good chance they would be captured!

Gen. Patton used the old log chain idea, saying, "Trying to lead men from behind makes you a driver and not a leader. It is easier to lead men just as it is easier to drag a log chain. You cannot push a log chain and you cannot push troops. The troops will keep running back to you for instructions—really from fear. A leader must be up front. You got to know what is going on! You cannot swim without being in the water, and you cannot ice skate without being on ice. No one ever learned how to ice skate from a map board. Take the map with you and get up front and see if the map is correct."

There is a story about Gen. Patton which I have learned was not fiction. This is the story of Gen. Patton crossing a river. Gen. Patton returned to his headquarters to find his engineers pouring over maps trying to decide where to cross the river. Gen. Patton asked, "Why not cross the river at this point?" He pointed to a spot on the map and marked the spot with a red marker pencil.

The senior colonel answered, "We have little information about the depth of the river and the soil conditions at the point you marked."

"We will cross where I made the mark. Every man can walk across. Send a few tanks across to find out about the soil conditions. The banks are solid and the river bottom seems firm. The river is wide at this point, but is quite shallow."

"How can we be sure, General?"

"How do you think I got my pants wet? Right up to here is as high as the water is deep!" He pointed to the high water marks on his legs.

NEVER MAKE A DECISION TOO EARLY
OR TOO LATE

In a staff meeting some new officer would say, "I am proposing that we include this new National Guard Division with our training on the range."

Patient as he could be, Gen. Patton would ask, "When is that division supposed to arrive in the desert, Colonel?"

"I'm not sure."

"Then why should we make decisions now on their training? It is possible they may never arrive."

"It should be our standard policy!" the Colonel would explain.

Gen. Patton would give his lecture on decision making, saying, "There is a right time to make every decision. Trying to select the right time is the most important factor for every decision. It is a mistake to make the decision too early, and it is a mistake to make the decision too late. Every old maid will agree with me! The longer the decision can be delayed, the more facts we can collect on how to make the best decision. When the time is right and when we have the facts, we should never hesitate. To make a decision too early will result in too many changes. To make the decision too late results in too many emergency situations. We do not want to create any emergency situations which the enemy can use against us. If we plan carefully, we will never have an emergency."

This was in 1941 or about twenty years before the management experts invented the new decision making process called, "PERT," for Program Evaluation and Review Techniques. In 1941 Gen. Patton perfected this process with his own four letter words!

I can imagine what Gen. Patton would say about the new invention of "MOB," for Management by Objectives. He would explode, "What in hell were management experts doing before they managed by objectives? Did they try to run a corporation without any objective? Without any rudder? Didn't they know where in hell they were going? Every man must know the objective at all times."

NEVER MAKE A DECISION TOO EARLY
OR TOO LATE

Gen. Patton gave the MBO lectures before the letters were ever used. I remember his saying, "No man can do anything without knowing what he is doing! We got to let the American soldier know what he is fighting for and why. When we let him know what has to be done, he will do it. No soldier in the world can match the American soldier for getting the job done. Generals and staff officers do not win wars. Soldiers win wars! The soldier must know what he is trying to do. He must know the mission!"

The mission was all important and the objective had to be obtained at all costs even the loss of lives. Gen. Patton would stress, "It's all right to return from the fighting at the front." He would pause without smiling before saying, "But you had damn well better be on a litter and coming back feet first. I will shoot any man I see turning his back on the enemy unless he has been shot and falls over backward. I got a medal for saying I would shoot any man who turns back. That was in World War I."

Gen. Patton would not delay making a decision when it was time to make it. He would caution, "When a decision has to be made, let's make it. There is no totally right time for anything. There will always be good reasons for delays, but do not delay making a decision with the hope that it will go away! Get all the facts and make the decision when it has to be made."

TOO MUCH IF'N, PERHAPS'N
AND MAYBE'N WILL NEVER WIN A BATTLE

Gen. Patton made his staff exert every effort to get all of the facts before making a decision. In addition, he always placed a time limit on when the collection of facts had to be finished. When the decision hour arrived, there was no delay or hesitation. When the best available facts **were** reported, he had a few simple sentences which he used frequently to impress upon us the necessity of deciding what to do. He would say, "This may prove to be something other than the best, but we will do what has to be done. We will go with what we have got."

When Washington would send an order, Gen. Patton might protest, argue, and attempt to change what he believed to be an improper order. When the final word was received he would say, "Whether we like it or not, that is the way it is going to be. We will go with it."

I remember a colonel from a National Guard unit that Gen. Patton retired without any perhaps'n or maybe'n. I had been spending time in our Army regulations trying to decide what I should do with a National Guard colonel. The problem was given to me as Judge Advocate by the company commander of our Military Police company.

This National Guard colonel was a newly commissioned political officer who wanted to go to war, but he wanted to do it in style! He wanted all of the privileges of the rank without any of the inconvenience. The facts were that the colonel spent his nights in an air conditioned motel in Indio, California and commuted every day in an Army staff car. No complaints could be lodged against his National Guard military organization. The officers and the men were well trained. Unfortunately, the Governor of the home state had assigned a political friend to an important military position. This was not unusual in World War II after Pearl Harbor. Everyone wanted to be a colonel!

The National Guard troops attempted to comply with all of their colonel's orders. They maintained his air conditioned trailer which was far from our headquarters.

TOO MUCH IF'N, PERHAPS'N
AND MAYBE'N WILL NEVER WIN A BATTLE

They took food to the woman in the trailer thinking it was the colonel's wife. Since she was a shapely and attractive young woman, none of the troops hesitated to visit the colonel's trailer. During the heat of the desert sun the colonel spent his time with this woman in the trailer. All official papers and office work were brought to the trailer. At night the colonel drove to Indio and spent the night with the second wife. No one knew which woman, if either, was the proper wife!

The colonel told his staff that he would stay full time in the desert when he could be assured that every morning he would have a quart of milk and a morning paper on his trailer step! The milk had to be iced! The National Guard troops could make the delivery of the iced milk, but the morning newspaper was a problem which could not be solved. We were seventy miles from Indio and over a hundred miles from Los Angeles.

I was advised of the problem when the Military Police discovered the civilian trailer in our maneuver area. The MP's had also checked on the Army staff car which remained in Indio all night every night. It was hot in the desert. Despite the heat, no one had any air conditioning. Gen. Patton's tent was as hot as any of the tents for the troops. The Captain of the MP Company asked me how he could move the woman in the trailer because he was fearful for the safety of the woman living alone in the trailer at night.

We called in the staff officers of the National Guard unit for a conference. They were loyal to their Commanding Officer, but it was apparent they were not proud of their colonel's standard of living. They confirmed the milk and newspaper order.

I advised the Military Police that the only charge which I could use was the broad general charge of "conduct unbecoming an officer and a gentlemen." We could have suspicions that the colonel was having intercourse with one or both of his women, but the proof had to come from the women, always a doubtful source of proof if the women were "well cared for."

No order had been issued that every officer live in the desert. I could not charge the colonel with disobeying an order. National Guard officers were appointed and commissioned by the governors of the states. National Guard troops and officers came under federal, or control by the United States Army, only when the troops were called to active military duty by the President of the United States. This National Guard unit was on active duty with the U.S. Army. I discussed this problem with our Chief of Staff, the first officer under Gen. Patton. Before we could decide on a definite plan of action, some battalion commander asked Gen. Patton if he could get an air conditioned trailer and bring his wife to camp.

"Hell no!" was Gen. Patton's prompt retort.

"Then whose wife is in the trailer about twenty miles from here back near the base of the Chocolate Mountain range?"

Gen. Patton had never seen the trailer. The Chief of Staff asked our Military Police Company Commander to give a full report on the facts. When he finished his report, Gen. Patton ordered, "Williamson, you are Judge Advocate! Get that SOB court-martialled!"

I had to reply, "General, we have never published any order that every man must live in the desert without a wife. We cannot charge him with disobeying an order. The only charge I could write would be under 'conduct unbecoming an officer and a gentleman.'"

Some officer in the back of the room said, "I would say this SOB is becoming quite a gentleman!" Gen. Patton did not laugh when the staff laughed.

The Chief of Staff suggested, "Those National Guard colonels are a problem since they have political ties with the governors who have influence in Washington."

TOO MUCH IF'N, PERHAPS'N
AND MAYBE'N WILL NEVER WIN A BATTLE

"Are we sure of all the facts? Are you sure this woman in the desert is not his sister? Could it be this newspaper and milk delivery thing is merely latrine rumor stuff?"

"General, we cannot check which woman is the wife and which one is the sister, but we do know that he spends his nights in Indio with one woman and his days in the trailer with the other woman. He has never been in the field with his troops," the Military Police Captain answered.

"Williamson, how about unauthorized use of an Army vehicle?" Gen. Patton asked.

"This National Guard unit came to us with their own staff cars. It is the Colonel's vehicle. He can do anything he wants with it until we order something to the contrary. It would not be an easy case to make," I replied.

Gen. Patton asked again, "What trouble can we get into if we haul that woman and trailer into Indio?"

As usual, I had to make a decision promptly, "No legal trouble unless we should have an accident on the highway. No one should ride in the trailer when it is on the highway."

"Then I am going to retire that SOB!" Gen. Patton exclaimed. "Captain, hook a jeep onto that trailer. Put the gal in one of our ambulances. Put two military police cars with red lights and sirens screaming. Put one siren in front and one in back of the ambulance to prevent any chance of an accident. We will take this colonel and his 'sister' into town in the style to which they have been living. Do not exceed forty miles. Do this immediately."

The Captain asked, "What shall I tell the colonel?"

"Don't tell him anything! I want to see that SOB myself. I will put him in the ambulance! When I get through with him he will retire from the National Guard for physical disability. When I get through with him he may have cause for being physically disabled. I may kick the hell out of him!"

TOO MUCH IF'N, PERHAPS'N
AND MAYBE'N WILL NEVER WIN A BATTLE

There was no if'n, maybe'n or perhaps'n about Gen. Patton's decision. He had done what had to be done. Such quick decisions were not the usual rule with the politically appointed National Guard Officers. Under different commands many high ranking officers went on maneuvers with fancy air conditioned trailers and wives to soothe them after a hard day in the field! I remember the staff discussions about this improper conduct during the Louisiana maneuvers. The discussion was usually dismissed with the words, "If this gets too bad, we may have to do something."

Gen. Patton did not delay when action had to be taken. Often some new officer would suggest a delay saying, "This does not seem to be the right time to..."

Gen. Patton would break in saying, "There is no right time for anything! We will do what has to be done!"

After Gen. Patton finished with his attack upon the colonel with the National Guard, the colonel decided to retire from military service. We never received a protest from either wife, the governor of the state nor any politician in Washington.

NO GOOD DECISION WAS EVER MADE
IN A SWIVEL CHAIR

Our staff meetings would last an hour longer if some staff officer would say, "Our decision in this matter is based on the assumption that..."

Gen. Patton would interrupt, "Whoa! Hold Up! We do not assume anything. Why can't we get the facts so we do not have to assume?"

If the staff officer could give a valid explanation, Gen. Patton would be satisfied. If not, it would be a day the officer would never forget. Constantly Gen. Patton preached, "Get all of the facts. We must have facts to make decisions. A decision which is not based on facts is no decision at all! No good decision was ever made in a swivel chair! Get out of the chair and get the facts! Know on what facts you base your decision."

There would be some laughter. Patton would continue, "I mean it! No good decision was ever made in a swivel chair! Better to have a decision made on horseback than in a swivel chair. A man in a swivel chair does not have his juices going right. Nothing is going to his brain after the first twenty minutes in that chair. All of his brains will be down in his shoes. Get out of the swivel chair and know what is going on!"

One day a colonel was under attack from Gen. Patton. The colonel explained, "General, we cannot predict the weather. We must assume average weather conditions."

"No!" Gen. Patton countered, "We must assume the worst weather conditions and plan accordingly."

The colonel tried to cover, "We might wait a few hours before the launch."

"Then why are we trying to make that decision now. Have you contacted our "weather makers" - the men who tell us all about what is going to happen? What do they say?"

"I have not contacted them. I just assumed average weather."

"We have men's lives hanging on our decisions! We cannot assume anything. Whether we are in the desert or actual combat we must get the facts. How are you going to feel when you make a decision and several hundred men are killed? You want to try assuming that they are not dead? Never forget, colonel, that the life you save could be your own!"

Gen. Patton wanted exact facts about everything involving an operation. He wanted the exact weight of a gallon of gas, hot and cold! He wanted his staff to know in seconds the number of gallons an Armored Division would require to move fifty miles. He wanted the exact weight of rations for one day, ten days, and any number of days he requested.

Gen. Patton said, "Let's never have to look at each other and say, 'If only we had known!' We will always know."

I remember one time when we did not give Gen. Patton all of the facts. If the Jap Navy had changed course in the Pacific, there would have been an amazing change in the history of World War II. In the summer of 1942, the Jap Navy had a large invasion force in the Pacific. Mexico had just declared war on Japan. When our G-2 Intelligence Chief reported the task force, Gen. Patton put every man into high gear to defend the lower California Bay.

Gen. Patton concluded, "There is a chance we may get at the enemy! Mexico is now in the war. Mexico cannot defend anything against the Japs. The beaches of the lower California Bay are superior for landing a large invasion force. A million men could be unloaded on those beaches. It would be easy to overrun Mexico. Los Angeles is only a short distance from Mexico. Orange County and Los Angeles produce most of our aircraft. Any fool knows that this would be the best objective for the Japs. If they could knock out our aircraft production and get a toehold in California, we are in for a long war. We must prepare to meet the bastards on the beaches of Mexico."

Our excitement did not decrease when the Jap task force appeared to be heading for Alaska.

"Alaska is not the objective! That is to throw us off. They will never land in Alaska. They will strike in Mexico. No war has ever been fought so close to the Arctic Circle. The devils will hit Mexico," Patton exclaimed.

We had all of the facts on Mexico. We knew the roads, the railroads, beaches, soil conditions, number of people in the towns — we had everything. Our Desert Training Center was less than a hundred miles from the northern tip of the California Bay. We were on such a tight alert no man slept in a bedding roll. Every man slept in uniform. The helmet was the pillow. If we had received orders from Washington to move towards Mexico, every man and every vehicle would have been moving in less than sixty seconds. In less than three hours, Gen. Patton wanted to be on those beaches to meet the enemy. We slept in our uniforms for three nights before Washington reported that the Japs had done the stupid thing; they had landed on the tip of the islands of Alaska.

One of the staff officers congratulated our ordinance chief, "You can relax now and stop worrying about the ammunition." We did not have ammunition for anything other than small arms, the automatic pistols! If the Japs had struck Mexico, it would have been an interesting battle. I am sure that when Gen. Patton learned of our ammunition shortage, it would not have changed his decision to move. He would have said, "We will scare the hell out of them until Washington can fly in the ammo!"

I am sure that we would have raced our few tanks up and down the beaches with sirens screaming and dodging in behind the sand hills so that the enemy would count the same tank dozens of times. We would have stirred up so much dust that no enemy commander would take a chance of trying to land against the total destruction so many tanks could give.

By the time the Japs discovered that the tanks could not fire, we would have been supplied from Washington. When we held a staff meeting to review our aborted plans to move to Mexico, Gen. Patton learned of the lack of heavy ammo. He said, "And I sat in my damn swivel chair and thought we were ready to fight!"

CHAPTER 6

PRINCIPLES FOR SUCCESS

127

THE WAY TO WIN IS TO NEVER LOSE

"We will win because we will never lose!" Gen. Patton would explain to the troops. "War is the greatest game of life! Most games are played for a certain length of time like four quarters in football or nine innings in baseball. Not so with war. We will fight until we win. We will never give in." Gen. Patton's logic was so simple every man could understand the message. The message was clear; Gen. Patton would not lose.

Gen. Patton gave a more detailed explanation of his philosophy in his tent. "There can never be defeat if man refuses to accept defeat. Wars are lost in the mind before they are lost on the ground. No nation was ever defeated until the people were willing to accept defeat. England is defeated. The only hope is that Churchill refuses to accept defeat. When people are willing to give their lives for their country, the only way a nation can be defeated is to kill every man, woman and child. In the history of the world this has never happened. Wars are lost in the mind. We will never admit to the troops nor to the enemy that we will ever accept defeat."

This thinking matches Gen. Patton's idea that the body is never tired. It is the mind that thinks tiredness. The mind can eliminate the tiredness of the body.

This principle may seem new, but it was mentioned in the Bible as Gen. Patton would explain, "There are several descriptions of death in the Bible, such as 'He gave up the ghost.' Many patients in hospitals die when they give up and accept defeat. I recall a man building his own coffin. When the coffin was finished the man died. I know of several men who have retired to build their dream homes. When the homes were finished, the men died. Man must have a battle in life if he is to live, but he will never be defeated if he will never give in to defeat."

Years later when I heard the words of Churchill's famous commencement address, I puzzled over who had the idea first, Gen. Patton or Churchill. Churchill's commencement address of nine words, "Never give in! Never give in! Never give in!" Gen. Patton and Churchill visited many times during the course of the first war. It is unimportant which man spoke the words first. The idea behind the words preserved England and helped Gen. Patton to many victories in World War II.

There are many examples of this simple idea in medical circles. The military amputation hospitals always repeated the story of the high jumper who lost a leg, but he refused to stop high jumping. The mind controlled the body! On one leg he could jump higher than he ever jumped with two legs. He hopped towards the high bar on one leg. It was the amputated leg which had always tripped the bar when he had two legs.

Patrick Henry gave this philosophy in 1776 when he said "Give me liberty or give me death."

NEVER LET THE ENEMY PICK THE BATTLE SITE.

Along with Gen. Patton's never-lose principle was the idea that we would always fight on our terms. We will never let the enemy pick the battle site. Gen. Patton would stress, "Now and then we may get caught in a trap. Not too likely because we will know more about what the enemy is doing than their own commanders. We cannot be trapped if we stay alert. The secret is to move fast and in a direction the enemy would never expect. The chance of loss is too great to fight a battle on a site which pleases the enemy. That causes the loss of hundreds of good soldiers. We will decide when and where we will kill the enemy."

This is a simple idea, but it works. It is as simple as "never dig a foxhole" where the enemy can bury you in your own grave. All of these principles made up the total philosophy of never defend, always attack. This principle is not new. The idea started in civil affairs in the year of 1215 when the people of England pointed their swords at their king and demanded the Magna Charta which gave the people the right to fight their legal battles in their own home towns. Prior to the Magna Charta the people had to fight their legal battles at any place the king demanded. This is a basic right of our legal system, the people must be tried in their own venue, their home county. Or they can change the venue if they believe they cannot have a fair trial in their home town.

The same principle works in civilian business circles. Surround a prospect with his own telephone, protective secretaries, and keep-things-the-same assistants and the sale of a new idea or product is impossible. Any good selling shots will be lost by a telephone call or an assistant who keeps the prospect's mind from hearing the salesman's argument. The place to sell the business prospect is at lunch or at dinner at a place selected by the salesman! The protective secretary and the no-change assistants cannot protect their home ground!

NEVER LET THE ENEMY PICK THE BATTLE SITE

I remember Gen. Patton's words about enemies and friends. "Now friends are great. Just wonderful! Friends are like good win. Get better with years. But you need good enemies same as you need good friends. Probably need enemies more than you need friends. You always know where your enemies are because you know they will always be shooting at you. Sad but true, only a few friends will always be loyal. The enemies to watch are the luke-warm friends. I should say the hot-warm to your face friends and cold to your back. These types cause people to say, 'protect me from my friends. I can take care of my enemies.' Sort out these luke-warm types. Make them enemies. Expose them for their turn-coat attitudes. God knows we have enough luke-warm types in the Service. Grab these types by the nose and kick them in the pants. Make them take a position on something. Try to get them to take a position on anything! Make them put up or shut up. You would be amazed at the number of officers who have never stood for anything other than a short arm inspection. We can differ with each other and still be good friends. You won't be my friend if you don't level with me always. The worst enemy is the one who acts like your friend to your face and turns out to be your enemy when your back is turned. These are the back stabbers. Don't ever try to keep these bastards happy. Trying to keep such types happy and friendly is a mistake! Same as being blackmailed. I have enemies and I am glad they are enemies. I know who and where they are, and I strike at them every time I get a chance. It is far better to lose battles with true friends than to win a battle with any enemy. There is no loss with true friends because you will always fight together again. There is no victory when you win with the enemy."

Gen. Patton paused, "Now all of that is for us as individuals. Or that is the way I feel about enemies. We must decide how to treat friendly troops, those of our own country or some foreign country. We must not treat them as we do the enemy, but we have to wait and see how they act when under fire. No other organization is going to fight as hard as we will fight. We must be prepared to find our flanks exposed because our friendly troops couldn't move as fast as we did. Don't count on friendly troops to do much more than bring up the mail!"

NEVER FIGHT A BATTLE WHEN NOTHING
IS GAINED BY WINNING

I remember Gen. Patton explaining, "So many battles are fought in war and in civilian life, and nothing is gained by the victory. Every battle we fight will result in a gain or we will not fight. We will never defend, we will always attack. In civilian life nothing is gained in fighting over what the weather will be or has been. There is no great gain in merely being right. To be right about an unimportant subject is unimportant. Nothing is gained by being right about who is the best football player. Of course, it is necessary to admit being wrong. How many fights you could have avoided when you were a kid if you refused to fight unless you gained something. I know, when we were kids we got into fights for the fun of fighting! War is not fun. We are not going to fight any battles for fun."

To make his points, Gen. Patton would switch from civilian life to war for his examples. He advised, "Now every time we get close to the enemy we can expect him to shoot. We want him to shoot at us! How else can we tell where he is if he does not shoot? We will find out where he is, and we will keep moving so we cannot be hit. We will never go straight at the enemy if there is an easier way. We have the speed to move behind enemy lines. It will be lonely behind the enemy lines, but that's where wars are won. The natives behind the lines will not shoot much because they will not have any heavy guns. If we get behind the enemy, they will not shell us because they would be hitting their own kinfolk. No soldier likes to fire into his hometown. We will go in and take whatever we have to take, but we will not waste time on taking any position we have to defend unless we will gain in killing the enemy. The quickest way to win a war is to cut the enemy away from supplies. We are self-contained. We have everything we need to last behind the lines for days. We can capture any gasoline we might need. We will not mind being lonely because we know we can fight our way back to friendly troops. The best plan is to raise hell until the friendly troops can come up to us. Nothing goes faster than success. When we have the enemy on the run, we will keep him running. Night and day we will drive and never stop. We will never rest when we are winning."

Gen. Patton would pause frequently and look at the staff to see if any officer wanted to object to his ideas. "We will keep driving whether we have rations or not. We can always eat our shoes, our belts, or each other. We will be like the horse cavalry. We will feed off of the land. We will capture food and gasoline from the enemy. Those poor devils will not have their own food. We will be eating it. They will think they have us surrounded. We will teach the bastards that to surround us is to make sure they will die. When we are surrounded we can fire in any direction and hit the enemy."

This principle of war was expressed in the Battle of the Bulge when the American troops were surrounded. The Germans demanded surrender and the American commander responded with the famous word, "Nuts!" With support from the air and Gen. Patton's drive to the rescue, the Germans learned that nothing was gained by surrounding American troops. With Gen. Patton attacking, the Germans were always alarmed. They never knew where he would attack.

Gen. Patton often supported his ideas by quotations from the Bible. I remember his quoting, "Don't cast your pearls among swine." It might be difficult to see how this applied in war, but I remember his saying, "If the battle is worth it, we will go in and win. If it isn't worth it, we are not going to get shot at without some reason. The Bible tells us not to cast any pearls among swine. I never saw a pig wearing a string of pearls! We will not waste any time on pigs. We will kill the enemy where he can be killed easily and where we will gain the most by winning. We will not kill for the mere sake of killing people. We will not waste any time on fighting the battles the enemy wants us to fight. We will fight on our terms and we will win."

NEVER FIGHT A BATTLE WHEN NOTHING IS GAINED BY WINNING

Gen. Patton concluded. "You see when we take on their best troops and knock hell out of them, the others will throw down their guns and quit. It is the military leaders that we must kill." Frequently Gen. Patton would express his personal wish that he could fight the highest enemy leader and the victor of the personal fight would settle the war. I remember his boyish grin when he would say, "Now don't worry. I will kill the bastard no matter how many times he hits me!" We all knew that Gen. Patton's pistols were to be used in killing the German general, Rommell.

Gen. Patton's predictions were correct. Pictures of World War II show thousands of German troops throwing down their rifles and surrendering when there were no American troops to accept the surrender!

SUCCESS IS HOW YOU BOUNCE ON THE BOTTOM

"In our great country, most any fool can be a great success at something. The problem with success is that it leads to failure! When you are on top there is no place to go but down." This type of thinking was given by Gen. Patton in small staff meetings or in his tent at night.

"Life is like a roller coaster. Life has its ups and downs. I've been up and down many times. Every time I get an award or win a victory, I expect to be shot at by my enemies — even by my friends. The whole problem with success is when you climb that ladder of success you have to step on the fingers of some of your friends who are trying hard just to stay even. Usually, people hate those who win more than the average amount of success — whatever average is! If you think men will scream at you for winning, God save you from the screaming wives! Every wife wants her husband to be a commander although she will not let him command at home. So when you ride the roller coaster of life to a high point, always be prepared for the down slope. This is one of the problems with we silly humans. We have not changed in the last ten thousand years and there is no chance that we will change in the next ten thousand."

It was from Gen. Patton that I learned the story of Benedict Arnold. Gen. Patton shocked me one evening, saying, "Damn fine commander that Benedict Arnold. He was too successful! He won too many victories. He turned into a traitor because of the Continental Congress!" Gen. Patton related the story of Benedict Arnold's black shield at the West Point Military Academy. "It hangs there as a memorial to a great officer who failed to learn that the first enemy always is our own Congress!"

After the war I researched the life of Benedict Arnold and the black shield at West Point. As usual, I learned that Gen. Patton was correct in all that he reported. Arnold **did** have a great military record. Arnold won battles in the Revolutionary War which he was not supposed to win.

Members of Congress had "reserved" some of the battles for their own native sons. The way to punish a winning commander is to delay his promotion and hold down on his pay. Congress skipped over Arnold on several promotions. As a result, Arnold lost faith in the ideal that the United States of America could become a great nation. Arnold reasoned that no country could become great when Congressmen were interested only in local interests and not in the welfare of the entire country.

It is fortunate that Gen. Patton's thoughts about Congress were never spoken in public. I remember some of his remarks about Congress. "Congress is usually void of leadership. I don't know that Congress will ever have any leadership because they are always running for reelection. But don't worry about Congress. Just remember we have to live with them. Trying to get reelected every two years breeds great jumpers and not great leaders. Congressmen and senators are quick to jump on a horse and ride off in a direction they think the people might be going. If a congressman jumps on a horse going in the wrong direction, he will change horses in a hurry and try to jump at the head of the parade going in some other direction. Great leaders will always lead. A great leader will never try to jump up to the head of a convoy of troops or even public citizens."

Gen. Patton made further comments about Benedict Arnold, "Don't make the same mistake that Benedict Arnold made. Don't give up serving our Country no matter how many promotions or pay hikes you miss. Always remember we do not serve Congressmen. We serve a great Country. Remember that! We will be a great Country despite all that Congress might do! Try to understand that a congressman does not lose any votes by attacking the Army in peacetime. Heaven knows I understand this! After World War I the Army was cut to shreds, and I served for years without any promotions."

Some officer asked, "What do you mean by Country, General?"

"Good question! I don't know what a Philadelphia lawyer might say, but I know what I mean by Country. It is the Constitution! 'Just the greatest document ever written by man' according to an English Prime Minister. You know why we serve the Constitution? Simple! Recall what you said when you got your first commission or got a promotion. You take an oath to God 'to support the Constitution against all enemies foreign and domestic.' We are fighting for our great Constitution. We are not fighting for any man, president, senator, congressman nor potentate. This is what I mean by Country. Does this answer your question?"

"Yes, sir, General."

Gen. Patton continued, "When you get mad at some Senator or Congressman remember Benedict Arnold. He lost faith in the future of our Country. Of course, the Constitution was not written until several years after Benedict Arnold lost faith in our Country. If he had bounced off the bottom better, he would have been one of our greatest American Generals. He could not take the critics who were angry for his success!"

One evening I was with Gen. Patton and Col. Gay. Gen. Patton drifted around the Old and New Testament and commented on the Golden Rule. He reasoned, "Jesus was always trying to help the person who was down on the bottom of his luck. He never spent much time talking about those on the top of success except to tell them they should try to do something other than collect money. Preachers talk about the Golden Rule as if it was written to help their own church. Hell! The Golden Rule is not to make a great church or some super-perfect society of do-gooders. Jesus was interested in the little person who had lost all hope. You do unto others not for the sake of the other person but because the way you treat others is the way you are going to be treated. The Golden Rule should be, 'The way you do unto others is the way you are going to be done unto!' Remember Ben Franklin saying, 'If rascals knew how much money they could make by being righteous, the rascals would become righteous through pure rascality!' That's the Golden Rule! It makes us puzzle over whether we are rascals or righteous, doesn't it?''

I would go back to my tent and meditate over the truth which Gen. Patton had spoken. My tent mate was usually gone. With the other lieutenants, he would be in Indio or Palm Springs. These officers teased me about being an attorney, saying, "If you didn't have that law degree you would not have to stay after school with Gen. Patton." I enjoyed the evening sessions with Gen. Patton but quite often I wished I could also make the trips to Palm Springs with the other young lieutenants.

Gen. Patton added to the Golden Rule with an explanation of the judge-not rule from the Bible, saying, "Don't try to judge others because the way you judge others is exactly the same way you are going to be judged. You call a man a crook, he is sure to call you a crook in return. We will get the same as we dish out. 'What we sow we are sure to reap' is straight from the Bible. Religion is not for society, nor should it be. Religion is for the individual. Jesus never spoke of any New Deal or any Great Society for man. He was always talking how the little guy could improve his position in life with his fellow man."

Gen. Patton would bring everything down to a common level with the words, "What do you expect when you hit the top? You think you should be almighty? Look what happened to Jesus. He was successful and they killed him! How can we expect to have anything any better?''

Gen. Patton cautioned, "Never forget that you may think you are defeated when it is only the body that is tired."

Everything he said was influenced by war. He said, "Being in the Army is like being in life, you cannot quit!

SUCCESS IS HOW YOU BOUNCE ON THE BOTTOM

The only way to get out of the Army or life is by death! When you hit the bottom, bounce back as high and as fast as possible. Remember when you are standing on two feet you can only kick with one foot. When you are flat on your back you can kick with two! People are damn funny. People love a successful man. They love to have a hero. And they love to take their hero and cut him into shreds. Seems to make the people stronger to cut their hero up. And they love to see a martyr— and there is nothing in between a martyr and a hero. I know. I have been both. People love the underdog. That is, they love the underdog until he reaches the top. They will enjoy cutting the top winner back down to their average size or lower. That's why I say it is how you bounce on the bottom that will tell whether or not you can take success."

ALWAYS KEEP SOMETHING IN RESERVE

This principle might seem to be in conflict with Gen. Patton's constant driving to exhaustion, but Gen. Patton always had something in reserve. His will to win was a reserve force which could win most any battle.

We never prepared any battle play without at least one alternate plan. We had to do all of the work for all of the plans so that the change could be made quickly and as easily as possible. In addition we had to have add-on plans which were to be followed when one plan was finished. Any plan for regrouping was done on the move.

In the Patton movie, the scenes of the Battle of the Bulge were not overplayed. The situation with the Allied Forces was extremely grave. One of our large military forces was completely surrounded by Hitler's last hard-core troops in a desperate attack to avoid defeat. The weather was nothing but snow, wind, and bitter cold. In the movie, Gen. Eisenhower was with his highest military commanders, and asked "We have several hundred men holding out against the enemy. If these troops surrender, the enemy can get through our lines and cause havoc. We cannot supply anything from the air because of the bad weather. We must get ammunition and food to these besieged troops. How soon can you move to get relief to these troops?"

Gen. Patton answered, "The Third Army can start moving the minute I put through a call to my Chief of Staff, Gen. Gay."

Gen. Patton's superiors and fellow officers laughed at such a foolish statement. All of the other Field Armies were fighting the weather with little thought of fighting the enemy.

Gen. Patton answered their laughter saying, "We knew we would be called. Let me have a field telephone!"

Gen. Patton placed the call, and the Third Army did move instantly. The Battle of the Bulge Commander answered the demand for surrender by saying, "Nuts!" The weather cleared and Hitler's last major attack was turned into defeat.

After the war I talked with Gen. Gay about this scene in the Patton movie. I remember Gen. Gay's comments, "It was bitter cold. Patton ordered us to be ready to move when he went back to meet Gen. Eisenhower. You remember how tight the alert was when we were waiting to dash into Mexico? Well, it was the same in Germany except there was no sleeping on the ground as we did in the desert. We knew the enemy was preparing to strike. We did not know where. So Gen. Patton ordered several battle plans based on where he thought the enemy might strike. As you might know, his first battle plan was exactly where the enemy did strike. It was so cold it was no task at all to keep the men hugging together around the fires. Our camps looked like some shanty town with tarp shelters draped over the men. The wind was blowing so cold it was impossible to be exposed to the chill for more than a few minutes.

Every engine was started every few minutes to make sure it would be ready to roll the second we received the orders. I knew Gen. Patton would be calling so I was waiting in my trailer with open lines to all of the commanders. We knew we would be called by Gen. Eisenhower because we knew all of the other units would forget the war and be trying to fight the cold weather. The second Gen. Patton called and gave me the number of the plan, I held up one finger indicating plan number one. Before I finished talking, the engines were roaring so loud I could barely hear Gen. Patton. When the weather is that cold the men prefer to be rolling rather than sitting around a fire. We rolled through the German countryside and enemy positions without collecting much enemy fire. There was so much snow blowing the enemy could not tell but what we were German tanks!"

Many historians have written about Gen. Patton's ability to move men into combat. It is my opinion a greater talent was his ability to change battle plans quickly. I remember Gen. Patton's words at some of the briefing sessions, "We must be able to move around like a boxer. The faster we move the easier it will be to kill the enemy. If we cannot change battle plans, it's the same thing as digging a foxhole where the enemy will find us and put us in our graves. We have to be able to change or we will get the hell shot out of us, and we would deserve it! When we are not moving we are losing. Nothing ever stays the same in war."

Any commander or staff officer who would not make changes would be transferred. I remember one colonel insisting, "We have been doing it this way for years!"

"Then it is time we changed, colonel. We must be able to change any and all plans so the enemy will not know what we are doing. We must be able to change any hour of the day or night!"

Although Gen. Patton would drive to the last inch of supplies, there was at least one alternate plan in reserve.

REVENGE BELONGS TO GOD

There was never an hour in our lives with Gen. Patton that we were not building hatred for the enemy, but we never trained for revenge. Gen. Patton respected the enemy and admired some of the achievements of their generals. He never discussed destroying the enemy for the sake of revenge. The enemy was to be hated and destroyed as the only way to peace and self-preservation. It was seldom that Gen. Patton used the word revenge in any lecture or conversation. The soldiers of the enemy had to be hated and killed to save our own lives, but not as revenge for some previous act of the enemy. War was a game of life. Men had to be trained to win the war. Killing for revenge would not help win the war.

It was true that Gen. Patton would comment, "I cannot see any reason for taking any prisoners alive!" These words were to help build hatred for the enemy. The prisoners taken by Gen. Patton's men were treated better than most prisoners because Gen. Patton's men had better than average treatment.

I remember one conference when Gen. Patton stopped a full colonel in the middle of a sentence. The colonel stated, "We are low on supplies and gasoline. There is plenty available but Washington is not getting it to us fast enough. We are losing training time in the desert. We can slow our training and get even with Washington. If they cause delays we will show them how to really delay a program. We can get revenge by . . . "

Gen. Patton cut the colonel's conversation, saying, "Colonel, revenge belongs to God. We don't try to get revenge against anybody to get our supplies. If we can't get supplies, we will go with what we've got. If we go out for revenge, it could be we would never get our supplies. We will destroy our best efforts if we work on revenge. Revenge belongs to God."

Gen. Patton was silent for a moment before he smiled and added, "I am not at all sure that God could ever straighten out the problems of Washington, but He could do it better than we could."

The words, "Revenge belongs to God" were engraved in my mind. It would be several years before I discovered these words were from the Bible. This principle was a part of Gen. Patton's philosophy. It matched, "Don't fight a battle if you don't gain anything by winning." Nothing would be gained by merely getting revenge against the enemy.

Years later I remember this principle when I was under attack in civilian life by a political enemy who was using every trick in the book to destroy me and my professional reputation. There were many things which I could have done in revenge, but Gen. Patton's words restrained me. Early one morning my clock-radio awakened me with the news that my political enemy had hung himself. Revenge belonged to God! He settled the problem in a more severe fashion than I would have wanted. Gen. Patton's words lingered, "Leave a few things to God. You go out of your way for revenge, and you will destroy yourself!"

CHAPTER 7

PRINCIPLES FOR LIFE AND DEATH

GEN. PATTON LECTURING WITHOUT NOTES

GEN. PATTON ON GUNNERY RANGE – 1942
FIRST DAY TO WEAR PISTOLS

AUTHOR'S VIEW OF GEN. PATTON'S TENT

DESERT BASE CAMP HOME WITH SOLAR
HEATED WASH BASIN

DESERT HOME WHEN ON MANEUVERS

GEN. PATTON'S TENT AND CHAPEL SERVICE
note Gen. Patton, front row right

OFFICER'S QUARTERS IN THE DESERT
note latrine at the far end of the tents

WITH HIS MEN WITH SAME GRAVE AND MARKER

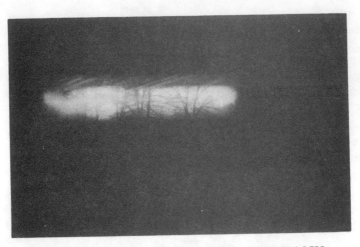

VIEW FROM A "BUTTONED-UP" TANK

ONE OF THE FIRST MEDIUM TANKS – 1942
NOTE NEW STYLE TANK HELMET

ONE OF THE DESERT BUGLERS

FORMATION FOR LOWERING OF THE FLAG

DEATH AND BURIAL, DECEMBER 21,1945

DEATH CAN BE MORE EXCITING THAN LIFE

Gen. Patton destroyed the fear of death with his deep religious faith and a keen sense of humor. He taught us to laugh at death. He pictured death as the greatest thrill of life. I am convinced that Gen. Patton was sincere when he stated that he prayed to God that he could be killed in combat. I remember his saying so often, "I would like to be killed by the last bullet fired at the last battle of the war!"

In the Patton movie several minutes were given to portraying Gen. Patton with a belief in reincarnation. Never in any discussions did I hear Gen. Patton talk of reincarnation. He did speak of the fact that there were no new battles to fight. Every form and type of battle had been fought in the thousands of years of our existence. There could not be any changes in the type of battle, only the weapons would change. I am sure that Gen. Patton had studied every battle reported in the history books. He spent his life visiting battlefields. For him to say as he did in the movie, "I've been on this battle field before" did not mean that he believed in reincarnation. It meant that he had studied the battle field in great detail and had walked the ground where the battle had been fought.

There was never any doubt in the mind of any soldier that Gen. Patton believed in God. Gen. Patton's religion was good for all seven days of the week. He did not confine his religion for show on Sunday although he did attend Sunday church services frequently with the troops. The first Sunday we were in the Desert Training Center, Gen. Patton ordered a church service. We didn't have a church! We didn't have any chairs, but we had church! All we had was an altar which was set in the desert sand in front of Gen. Patton's tent with the American flag. Standing erect on the front row for the first service was Gen. Patton!

Gen. Patton had respect for the army Chaplains and had them at staff meetings when important decisions were to be made. He was always calling on the Chaplains to "get a hot line to God!" During the Battle of the Bulge when the weather was so terrible, Gen. Patton ordered the Army Chaplain to write a prayer that would change the weather. This prayer for good fighting weather was cited in a previous chapter. The prayer asked "Restrain these immoderate storms, grant us fair weather for battle, graciously hearken to us as soldiers who call upon The, that armed with Thy power, we may advance from victory to victory and establish Thy justice among men and nations." Gen. Patton gave this prayer on Dec. 12, 1944. It took God a few days to clear the weather, and the soldiers did "advance from victory to victory."

. Gen. Patton's religious faith came through in his many references to death. Fear of death was under constant attack by Gen. Patton. "Did you ever stop to think how much more exciting death can be than life? We know what it is like to live on this earth. We do not know what it would be like to live after death. We know damn well there will be some life after death! Take a good look at nature." Gen. Patton's lectures about death gave us more confidence than sermons in church.

I was impressed with Gen. Patton's intimate knowledge of the Bible. This knowledge exceeded that of any of the several religious leaders I have known. One of his biographers said in a conference that Gen. Patton could identify by chapter and verse more quotations than any international Bible scholar. For Gen. Patton the Bible was a series of stories of combat.

I remember his explanation of fear and faith. We were nearing the longest day of the year, June 21, 1942. Col. Gay and I were on our way to the General's tent. There was a red glow in the western sky. As Col. Gay and I approached, Gen. Patton said, "Damn fine sunset. Makes you feel great just to see such a sight. Everything is in balance! Just perfect. Just like fear and faith. You get to having too much fear, you gotta find the faith to match the fear. You get more faith, you will get more fears to test your faith. God keeps you trying to conquer all fears to see just how much you can take. He will never give you more than you can conquer. Of course, you can always give up and fall down with your fears. But if you don't give up, you can destroy all of your fears. God runs both the fear and the faith departments. If there ever was a devil, God could whip him easily. God would not fail at anything! This would include killing the devil. Fear and faith grow together. If you don't have the faith to face death, not much chance you will have enough faith to live a full life. Would be like a whole life of living half dead!"

"You see all of that in the sunset, General?" Col. Gay asked.

"All that and more! Well, not really. I just see a small part of the universe, but anybody who could put this universe together had a great battle plan."

We watched silently as the sun changed the colors on the Chocolate Mountains of California.

Every soldier knew that Gen. Patton was concerned about him. If the soldier was afraid of death, there was no need to worry because Gen. Patton admitted being scared. Gen. Patton was as loyal to his men as they were to him. This devotion was difficult for strangers to understand. Strangers could not believe that men could be so loyal to a commander who was so hard and demanded so much. Gen. Patton demanded death for every·soldier if it was necessary for victory, but Gen. Patton would be the first to give his life.

The stories and the legends about Gen. Patton were unlimited even in 1942. I remember one newspaper reporter who told me he intended to write a story that would make a farce out of the Patton myth. This reporter was on the staff of a large national newspaper chain. How he managed to dodge the draft was a subject he would not discuss. It was my task to accompany this reporter during his visit to the Desert Training Center. We stopped our jeep to watch an angry rifleman who was jumping up and down on the starter of his motorcycle. This soldier seemed a good candidate for the reporter to question about the myth of all of the soldiers loving their Gen. Patton.

The newsman asked, "Do you think Gen. Patton will go to heaven when he dies?"

The reply was immediate. "He will if he wants to but not until he is ready!"

The reporter was intent on provoking some unfavorable comment about Gen. Patton. The reporter asked the rifleman, "Do you think it possible that Gen. Patton would go to hell?"

"Look! With Gen. Patton anything and everything is possible! If he decided to go to hell, I would sure like to go along!"

The reporter shook his head in disbelief. We returned to base camp.

There were many stories about Gen. Patton and the loyalty of the soldiers. They enjoyed his lectures, his humor, his laughing at himself and making them laugh with him. I always liked the story about a member of Gen. Marshall's staff who asked a second lieutenant if he believed that Gen. Patton could walk on water.

The lieutenant replied, "Colonel, I know Gen. Patton! If he had to walk on water, he would figure out a way and within twenty-four hours he would have me doing it!"

With all of these stories there was one about the soldier who was questioned, "You think your Gen. Patton is so great! Do you think he will arise from his grave after three days?"

"Hell no!" The soldier answered. "Anything he is going to do, he will do it in less than three days! Dead or alive he would never stay in a foxhole for three days."

One of the lectures which I remember was the one about heaven. Gen. Patton said, "We know little or nothing about heaven. It is supposed to be the best of everything. If so, why should men be so scared to die? God can whip the devil any day of the week. Any power that can put this universe together can do everything. I am amused at those preachers who stand in the pulpit and preach about the glories of heaven, but they are scared of death. Give these types a slight pain and they may die from fright! If heaven is so great, why would such types be afraid to die? Looks like they would welcome a chance to get into heaven and get out of earth! Why do they hesitate? One thing I know, death is going to be something!"

He gave his usual smile and continued, "At least death will be different than life. I am sure that death will be exciting because it is only a phase in the cycle of life!"

BETTER TO FIGHT FOR SOMETHING IN LIFE
THAN DIE FOR NOTHING

Gen. Patton laughed at death and the men laughed with him. His talks to the troops provoked laughter but his messages were remembered.

"We are lucky people. We are in war! We have a chance to fight and die for something. A lot of people never get that chance! Think of all those poor people you know that have lived and died for nothing. Total lives spent doing nothing but eating, sleeping and going to work until the gold watch is received. We are damn lucky to be fighting a war that will change history. If we live, we can put our grandchildren on our knees and tell them how we did it! If we die, our friends can tell how we died to make life better for them. If you are going to die, might as well die a hero. If you kill enough people before you die, they might name a street after you." The troops laughed. Whether the logic was reasonable or not, the men remembered every word.

Gen. Patton never gave the usual commander's pep talk such as "If we keep alert, we will all get out of this. Don't take any chances. We have lived through this before, and we will make it through this one."

Such words were not for Gen. Patton. He gave the harsh brutal truth. "Some of us are going to die. We are tough enough to take a dozen of the enemy when we go. We can be sure they cannot kill all of us. As long as any one of us remains alive, we will keep killing the bastards. Our chances of living are better in war than in driving on the highways. We can get killed on the highway and be dead for nothing. I would rather be shot through the head with an enemy bullet than to have my head bashed into a car windshield. When we are killed in war, we will always be remembered. We will never be heros for being killed on the highway. When we can take life and death and not get scared of either, we can whip anything."

Today, I presume, some would say that Gen. Patton brainwashed his men. If his training was brainwashing there are many who could use the washing system.

BETTER TO FIGHT FOR SOMETHING IN LIFE
THAN DIE FOR NOTHING

Helping people face life and death follows the basic laws of nature. There is no brain wash in Gen. Patton's words "Every day of life is one day closer to death." This is a cold hard truth. Most of Gen. Patton's principles are cold basic facts. Gen. Patton stressed the basic truth of war. "If we do not kill the enemy, the enemy will kill us." This was a truth which many who preached for peace did not want to accept.

The troops laughed when Gen. Patton said, "If you see you are going to be killed, you might as well kill a dozen of the bastards before you go." His timing on such speeches was perfect. He continued, "You may not get killed. You might only get a bullet someplace where it would merely improve the circulation in your system! For that you would get the Purple Heart Award. Get hit three times and you get three medals! You get enough medals it will make you stronger just to carry them around!" When he gave this lecture his left chest was loaded with the many awards which he had received including the Purple Heart. You will only die once in this command. The draft dodger and the coward will die a thousand times every day of his life!"

This last thought was not originated by Gen. Patton, but he supported the thought with the cold naked truth. He always faced truth, grabbed it by the nose. I remembered Gen. Patton's words when I was with twelve new combat fighter pilots on a train to Florida from Williams Field, Arizona. We had been screened carefully to be a new breed of pilot, night fighter pilots. I was the senior officer of the twelve. We had been screened with super physical examinations and eye tests for the special night vision which was required. We would be using airborne radar, something that was so secret we were unable to gain even a slight bit of information. Every one of us had volunteered for the new program. Some of the tests had nothing to do with vision or physical ability such as sitting alone in a totally darkened box for half an hour. One thing we knew, we were going into the unknown.

BETTER TO FIGHT FOR SOMETHING IN LIFE
THAN DIE FOR NOTHING

On the train a young pilot came to me with a problem about his local draft board: It seemed the draft board wanted to draft him for military service! The young man's local draft board had him listed as physically unfit for military service. So the young man had driven into another state and enlisted. Since the draft boards had quotas to fill, the two draft boards were fighting over which draft board would get credit for the enlistment. As we discussed the problem I discovered that every one of us could secure exemption from military service for physical disability. We laughed at the last line on the physical examination form where the doctors had tagged all of us with the words, "denies all else" in answer to the question, "Other illnesses or disabilities!"

We coined a slogan for our group with the words, "Denies all else." It was not unusual for one young pilot to ask another, "Hey, dummy! Are you going to deny all else?" We laughed at how we had fooled the doctors. Today, I am not sure we fooled the doctors. The doctors knew we were going on difficult and unknown missions. They knew they had to select pilots who wanted to fight for something.

NEVER LET DEATH CATCH YOU IN BED

"More people die in bed than in war!" Gen. Patton explained. "Going to bed is like digging a foxhole. It is easy for death to catch you asleep. The Lord said, "Pick up your bed and walk!" Staying in bed is the same as staying in a swivel chair too long. The brain gets clogged and the body gets sick. Next thing you know some doctor will load you up with pills that are supposed to get everything back in order. Just moving around could do more good for you than a whole handful of pills."

The men laughed. On the staff we thought Gen. Patton was pushing too far. This was in 1942. Many years later doctors would start having their surgical patients "pick up their beds and walk" a day or two after surgery. From his knowledge of the Bible, Gen. Patton preached this practice more than thirty years before the medical profession started the walking treatment.

I never appreciated the impact of Gen. Patton's ideas until I visited nursing homes after the war. These nursing homes reminded me of Gen. Patton's words, "Dash out and meet death on your own terms!" It would be many years before society would start thinking that perhaps people should have the right to die on their own terms and not be nursed near death for twenty years as a vegetable. The heavy dosages of sleeping pills keep the senior citizens as immobile as potted plants.

I remember Gen. Patton saying "A lot of people die at forty but are not buried until thirty years later. Many people have a short tour with an illness and give up or die at an early age. They go from doctor to doctor until death catches them in bed.

Gen. Patton always preached that if you didn't keep moving around the juices would never get to the right places. Gen. Patton's death was not from a broken neck resulting from an auto accident. He died from the accumulation of liquids in his lungs and heart. The juices were not going to the right places. God has my sympathy for the wrath of Gen. Patton for his death in bed.

NEVER LET DEATH CATCH YOU IN BED

Medical science has advanced rapidly, but there is no pill as strong as Gen. Patton's advice, "Settle with death on your own terms!" So many people die young and are buried old. So many of us are so afraid of death that we never live.

FEAR KILLS MORE PEOPLE THAN DEATH

When I first heard Gen. Patton say, "Fear kills more people than death," I smiled because I did not catch the full impact of his words. When I heard these words later I noticed that the troops were silent. I puzzled over how many men understood what he was saying. No minister I have ever heard ever put life-after-death in such simple and blunt terms.

Today when I quote this principle, many people think the principle is as foolish as I did when I first heard it. One man retorted to me, "Death is death, isn't it?"

But death was not death for Gen. Patton. With the faith to destroy fear, death would be a phase in the cycle of life. Much of Gen. Patton's total philosophy is in the words "Those in fear will die a thousand deaths." I remember Gen. Patton saying, "A coward is always in hell because he will suffer a thousand deaths every day. A brave man will only die once!" He explained further, "When you have the faith to fight for something to death, there is no death. Death will be only a phase in the cycle of life."

The soldiers told many stories about what would happen when Gen. Patton died. Every soldier knew that Gen. Patton wanted to give his life in combat. We loved him because he was so concerned about all of us. No one expected him to live forever. The stories about his death started years before the fatal accident.

According to one story, Gen. Patton died and demanded that St. Peter tell him where he could locate God. In the presence of God, Gen. Patton exploded, "What in the name of hell is the idea of having me killed in an auto accident? I asked and prayed to you to take my life in combat. How unthoughtful of you to pick me off in a stupid auto accident. What kind of a death is that for a soldier? Give me orders to go to hell! I cannot face my own brave soldiers who have earned their places in heaven."

God answered, "If you want to go to hell, it can be arranged!"

Gen. Patton saluted, clicked his heels, did a sharp about face and walked away.

God called to him, "Gen. Patton, on giving your request serious thought, I wish you would reconsider and stay with us."

Gen. Patton protested, "I do not belong here. I am going to hell!"

God pleaded, "I don't want you to go to hell. I want you here with us. If you go to hell, it will be only a few weeks until you will destroy the devil, put out all the fires of hell, and my people will leave heaven to be with you. Please stay, for Heaven's sake!"

Gen. Patton hesitated so God added, "And we will let you wear your uniform any time you wish!"

There was another story about Gen. Patton's death which the soldiers enjoyed telling before his death. The story was: Gen. Patton died and pressed the doorbell of the gates of heaven. When no one answered, he pounded on the door with his fist. St. Peter finally arrived dressed in toga and sandals.

Gen. Patton exploded, "Why weren't you at the gate? Don't you know your assigned duty? Didn't you ever read the Bible. You know you belong at this gate twenty-four hours a day. What kind of uniform is that? Did I disturb your sleep? Look at your feet! You could never run a mile in those frail sandals. What happened to your razor? Or are you growing a mosquito breeding ground with that beard? Where is your necktie? Where is your helmet?"

The stories were endless. The laughter of the troops displayed the total devotion of the troops to their commander.

Gen. Patton's thoughts about death were not unlike those of Churchill who said in 1941, "It is a good time to live and a good time to die." This matched Gen. Patton's thought that both living and dying could be exciting.

FEAR KILLS MORE PEOPLE THAN DEATH

I remember Gen. Patton's remarks about fear. "Fear makes us stronger. Every time we whip a fear we will get a bigger fear. We can take any fear if we are not fearful of death. One thing is sure we will all live until we die. Some of us die from fear but our breathing could go on for years. There is more to life than breathing. Death has to be the best part of living!"

"Our big problem is we do not understand life after death. The whole joy of life is taking chances to build enough faith to destroy all of our fears. That is why gambling is so much fun. The highest form of gambling is combat with an enemy that wants to kill you. You bet your life on the gamble. It is your life or the life of the enemy. You can never gamble any higher stakes! If we didn't have wars for men to gamble on, we would have something else. We are all gambling that we can push death aside until we get ready to die. Fears make us try harder. It is the same as racing fast cars or speed boats. It is the risk or fear that makes the chase exciting. It is always more fun to be in the chase or the gamble than to make the catch. War is the greatest thrill of life because the soldier has the greatest risk. It is the highest form of gambling every day. It is more fun to chase and destroy the enemy than to sit in fear in a foxhole and wait for the enemy to blow you into kingdom come!"

With Gen. Patton's assistance I was transferred to the Army Air Corps for flight training. We were losing pilots at a rapid rate in Europe. Every soldier who could pass the physical for flight training and was under twenty-seven was drafted for flight training. Since the Armored Corps was younger in service than the Air Corps, there were no pilots in the Air Corps who had ever been in an Armored organization.

As I have reported earlier, I remember so well the last night in Gen. Patton's tent. Col. Gay walked to the tent with me. As we approached, Col. Gay said, "I am anxious to know what the General is going to say to you."

I remember one remark which Gen. Patton made. "Now remember, we need each other. Don't forget us when you are up there and we are fighting on the ground. Try to pour your fire on the enemy and not on our tanks!"

We discussed the Carolina maneuvers and the capture of Gen. Drum. This last night was one of the few times that we discussed our first meeting on the bridge in Carolina. I confessed that I had intended to reprimand that tank driver for being on the bridge. Gen. Patton commented, "You would have been wrong if you had not reprimanded me. You were in a higher headquarters and the rules of the maneuver did say that no tank should ever cross on a bridge."

Col. Gay had never heard the full story of the capture of Gen. Drum. Gen. Patton related the story and laughed at the anger of Gen. Drum when captured.

After graduation from flight training I was assigned to the Night Fighter Pilot program. About two years later my leg was amputated and my military career was ended. I did not hear from Gen. Patton until a few days after Sept. 30, 1945, the day he was removed from command of his great Third Army. He wrote to me on Sept. 24, 1945. In the letter he stated as follows:

> Many thanks for your good letter of 13 September. I am, unfortunately, completely unable to make any commitments for the future at this time as I have no idea when I shall again be in the United States. With all good wishes on your return to civilian life, I am,
>
> Very truly yours,
> G. S. Patton, Jr., General.

In my letter of Sept. 13, 1945, I asked that he visit Indiana to receive the tribute which he had earned. I was amazed that the reply was received in less than ten days from the time I had written. Several years later I learned how despondent Gen. Patton had been when he wrote the letter. The typing indicated that he had not used a stenographer. Gen. Patton never returned to the United States. About sixty days after Gen. Patton wrote to me, he was riding with Gen. Gay. They were in a minor auto accident. The accident was minor, but Gen. Patton's neck was broken. Gen. Patton died on Dec. 21, 1945. His burial was with his Third Army Troops in a cemetery in Luxemburg. The people of the world, including the enemy, mourned the loss of a great leader.

Several years later, Gen. Gay was stationed in Chicago as the Commanding General of the Fifth Army. Without an appointment or prior call, I stopped at the Fifth Army Headquarters and asked to see the Commanding General. The four stars of a general can change some men, but not a man of the great caliber of Gen. Gay. Within minutes I was in the General's office discussing our favorite subject, Gen. Patton. We looked at each other across his desk. Gen. Gay commented, "It has been a long time since we had our desks together so we had to look at each other all day. Seems a century since we were in the I Armored Corps and the Desert Training Center."

We discussed the death of Gen. Patton's Aide, Lt. Jensen, our personal friend. Gen. Gay talked of the problems with the campaigns through France and Germany. He talked slowly and reviewed every word before he spoke. This was his nature. He had known Gen. Patton for many years. They had played polo together. Gen. Gay had been Gen. Patton's Chief of Staff throughout all of the campaigns in Europe. I told him of receiving a letter from Gen. Patton in 1945. Gen. Gay said, "Gen. Patton mentioned he had received your letter. Except for his family, I suspect the letter he wrote to you was one of his last personal letters."

I stated that I was sorry to hear of Gen. Patton's auto accident and death. We put together the old story which the troops told of Gen. Patton reprimanding God for permitting him to die in an auto accident.

Gen. Gay started slowly, "You know . . ." He was silent for several minutes before saying, "I'm glad the General died when he did. God knew best. I am glad he died when he did."

I opened my mouth in shock.

Gen. Gay continued, "Don't get the wrong idea. I was as sorry for his death as any one because we lost a great man and a good friend. Let me explain why I said what I did. You know the General was killed on his way to a game reserve. The hunting trip was my idea. I thought a hunting trip in the country would give me time to talk to him away from his office. I wanted the General to retire from military service and return to the United States and receive the honors to which he was entitled. This was when he mentioned your name. He said you wanted him to return for some tribute from the state of Indiana. He did not oppose me on leaving the service, but he said he intended to resign and not retire. During his last days, his mind wandered over the many battles and campaigns. He refought many of the battles. You remember how he would shed big tears. Well, he cried when he recounted the thousands of lives that had been lost because of the gasoline shortages. Yes, we were short of rations, even maps! You see, the General was preparing to write a book about the war. He wanted to document the campaigns. He wanted to document the losses caused by the Allied Command and Congress with their playing the war like political chess at the cost of thousands of lives. I had to agree with all that he wanted to do. His conclusions were correct, but I did not want him to do it. Everything he wanted to say was true, but I did not want the General to get into such a battle. I reasoned with him that he could lose the favor of the American people. He argued with me and supported his arguments with the many political leaders who made the trip to Europe to ask him to run for President—both parties wanted him!

Gen. Gay paused, "Do you remember what he said about politicians when we were in the Desert Training Center?"

I answered, "It seems I remember him saying several times that he would never run for any public office."

"Yes, he said that often. But if he had lived he might have changed his mind. He was so intent on giving the truth to the American people. One thing that might have changed his mind was Ike's (Eisenhower) trying to keep the Senators and Congressmen from visiting our Third Army Headquarters to see Gen. Patton. Ike's office had to approve every visit. Well, if he had lived, he might have listened to some of these men. Honestly, I think he could have been elected President. God knows he had enough money to run a national campaign. With all of the General's wealth plus that of his wife and the friends in the east, he would have put on a huge campaign. I told him that it was my personal opinion that he was too honest for politics. You know he couldn't hold back from speaking the truth. Never could! I think he would have been miserable in politics, and I told him so."

Gen. Gay stopped. I mumbled, "I agree with you."

He listened, but didn't agree. "My only success was in getting the General to agree to this hunting trip."

We were silent for several minutes. The General would have been angry if he could have seen the tears rolling from my eyes. Gen. Gay turned his back to me. I could see him drying tears. He spoke with his back to me. "Well,

Williamson, God has my sympathy. I am sure he raised hell up there. I know he would have been one hell of a good President, but he would have had more grief than we had in the whole war."

In the silence that followed I knew there was something which I should say, but I didn't know what to put in words. I put a few words together saying, "He missed the down slope! Remember how he talked of preparing for the down slope every time the top of success was reached. I agree with your thoughts, Gen. Gay, but I would have enjoyed having a chance to visit with him. I am glad he died at the top of his success."

Again we were silent. Gen. Gay broke the silence, "The longer I am in the States, the happier I am that Gen. Patton never returned to see our society today. He would have attacked every politician in office!"

A secretary came in for the third time to say that they were holding important long distance calls. I left because we were in tears.

My memories of Gen. Patton and his principles have influenced my life. Twice I have been sentenced to death by doctors. I remembered his words, "Death can be exciting! Live until you die. If you can take death you can enjoy life!"

Many times I have turned away from community, political, church and family feuds because "nothing would have been gained by winning."

I fought some battles with government officials who failed to remember that the people of the United States are sovereign. To quote a Patton Principle, "I killed a few skunks in the government who were digging under the front porch of our house, the Constitution."

When I won a battle and was ready to be attacked by my enemies, I remembered Gen. Patton's words "When you are on top there is no place to go but down."

FEAR KILLS MORE PEOPLE THAN DEATH

I am proud of the hours I spent with Gen. Patton, much of the time in his tent in the dusk of the evening. I remember so often the discussions of the difference in killing an enemy in combat and taking the life of a fellow citizen in a criminal prosecution. Gen. Patton questioned me about my criminal prosecution work representing the state of Indiana before entering on active duty with the Army.

I remember Gen. Patton asking, "Do you have to hate a man to prosecute him in court?" We agreed that in combat or in the courts it was a duty which had to be done whether with hate or without hate. We discussed the methods of how to turn men off from killing when the war was over. We agreed tht it would be a problem to change killers into peace-loving citizens.

In World War II, the world needed a commander who knew that war meant killing people. Gen. Patton was that commander. For Gen. Patton, war would never be a political battle, a cure for unemployment, a chance for political office, or a cure for the local economy. War meant people had to be killed. The quicker the enemy could be killed, the quicker the war would be over.

Gen. Patton is receiving the tribute from the world which he deserves. The Patton movie is used to instill courage in the White House, to build spirit in football teams and to train military cadets.

Major General H. Essame, An English officer in his book, **Patton, A Study in Command**, said, "Never in the history of war is there such an instance of a single army having such a great effect in deciding the major issues of a campaign. Third Army's record is peerless by any measure." Gen. Patton accomplished all of this despite all of the reprimands, the withholding of gas, the failure to adequately supply the rapid advances. Gen. Patton bounced from the bottom every time to win the war for those who wanted to tear him down from his high position of constant victories.

FEAR KILLS MORE PEOPLE THAN DEATH

Gen. Patton's most effective weapon was not the tank. It was the individual soldier who was trained to be totally fearless. Gen. Patton's men loved the thrill of combat and the ability to face death. Gen. Patton did believe that the greatest thrill of life was death. However, no man I ever knew was as soft as Gen. Patton. No officer or enlisted man I ever knew cried as many tears as Gen. Patton. For Gen. Patton, combat with the enemy meant an end to the killing of people on both sides. If he had not been restrained in his drives toward the heartland of Germany, the war would have ended many months earlier.

As Major General H. Essame said in his book, "Gen. Patton had opportunities which he was not permitted to follow—which would have proven decisive, shortened the war, saved thousands of lives, and left the West in a better strategic posture than it would be more than a quarter of a century later." The books which Gen. Patton wanted to write will be written by historians for centuries.

Gen. Patton trained the troops for a hatred for the enemy, but he was quick to soften and show compassion—to turn off the desire to kill. No one wanted the war to end as much as Gen. Patton. No general tried as hard to prevent the loss of lives on both sides. The war lasted much longer than necessary because the political leaders lost the "grip on the nose of the true enemy." Gen. Patton would fight and win because he would never give in to defeat.

When the war did end, Gen. Patton was the first to forgive the enemy. He was the first to attack the nose of the new enemy, the problem of bringing peace in Europe. He grabbed the nose of the problem at least thirty years before the political leaders applied Gen. Patton's principle of facing truth

Gen. George S. Patton, Jr. is buried in Luxembourg with his troops. He is buried in the same type of grave, with the same headstone and the same cross as every other soldier. No words on the cross state that Gen. Patton was the Commanding General of the Third Army. The crossarm states, "General 02605. 3rd Army." Gen. Patton, even in death, did not serve over his men; he served with them in life and in death.

Years after his death I talked with Major Gen. George S. Patton, the son, about the possibility of moving Gen. Patton's grave site to the United States. The son replied, "We have discussed this many times with the family. The grave site cannot be changed."

Although it is Gen. Patton's wish to be with his men, I regret that the greatest military commander of our history is on foreign soil.

All of Gen. Patton's principles came pouring into my mind when I was driving alone on an Interstate Highway in Oklahoma in 1975. By some quirk in the clouds and radio waves, I was receiving a radio station in Seattle, Washington. The radio announcer was interviewing a descendent of the Indian Chief, Seattle. The words of the Indian Chief were so like those of Gen. Patton that I wrote them down on a map so that I could remember the exact words. When I spoke the words I could see that Gen. Patton had packed the wisdom of the centuries into the Principles which he gave to the troops.

The words of Chief Seattle were "There is no death, only a change of life. The dead are not powerless!"

Gen. Patton is not dead! He has had a change of life. His principles will have power forever.

ACKNOWLEDGMENTS

I acknowledge my appreciation to so many for the encouragement to write **GENERAL PATTON's PRINCIPLES.**

The service clubs and organizations are as follows:

The Rotary Clubs of Tucson. Arizona and District Governors of Rotary, Don Ownbey, Fran Coffee, Henry Egbert and Earl Upham.

The Rotary Club of Green Valley, Arizona, with special appreciation to Robert McGhee and Everett Hardy.

The North Tucson Exchange Club and the club president, Gus Psaltis.

The Auditor's Club of Davis-Monthan Air Force Base, Tucson, Arizona.

The Tucson Women's Council of Realtors.

The National Contract Management Association of Phoenix, Arizona and St. Louis, Missouri.

The Tucson National Country Club with special appreciation to the lady who came to me after my address, saying, "Thank you for Gen. Patton's philosophy about death. I will always remember the words, 'Death is only a phase in the cycle of life.' I buried my husband last week. I am confident now that I can go on alone and stop crying."

ACKNOWLEDGMENTS

I want to give credit to the following for furnishing the photographs:
Major General George S. Patton III, the son of Gen. George S. Patton, Jr.
Kay Durban for photographs and also for information confirming the Benedict Arnold shield at West Point.
Col. Frank B. Tennant, Major Peter K. Friend and Capt. Michael C. Mandell, Dept. of the Army, The Pentagon, Washington, D. C.
John M. Purdy and John A. Campbell, Directors of the Patton Museum, Fort Knox, Kentucky.
The Presidio Press, San Francisco, California for the picture of the tank crossing the river.
Nina Ferris, the artist who did the touch-up work on the photographs.

ACKNOWLEDGMENTS

So many individuals have furnished information and encouragement. I am grateful to the following:

August F. Cordean, Director of Procurement, Fort Knox, Kentucky, for the dates of Gen. Patton's commands.

Charles M. Province, President of the Patton Historical Society, for the Gen. Patton journal articles.

Charles E. Dornbush for the text of the Gen. Patton speech to the Third Army.

Donald E. Houston, author of **Hell On Wheels**

William Sonneborne and James J. McLaughlin, editors of the South Bend Tribune, South Bend, Indiana for the articles about the soldier Gen. Patton slapped.

Bobley Publishing Co. and Standard Educational Corp. for the quote on health.

Gen. Essame of London, England, and Scribner's Sons, the author and publisher of **Patton, A Study in Command**.

Viola Gribanovsky for reviewing my rough notes.

Jack B. Jewett, E.D. Jewett and Gerry A. Bolkcom of the Arizona Territorial.

Robert C. Perry and Jan Loeseke for proofreading.

The descendant of the Indian Chief Seattle, for the words used in the last page of this book.

Howard R. Baker who shocked me into appreciating Gen. Patton's stature in history. Howard Baker touched my shoulder and said, "For me it is an inspiration to touch anyone who served with Gen. Patton."

To my wonderful wife and family for giving me so much to live for through military and surgical tours of duty in addition to the "tour of duty" of writing a book.

To all those who have given encouragement whose names I have missed in the haste of printing.

To all those whose faces appear in my photographs. I remember every face, but names are missing in my memory.

To all, to each and to everyone a special thank you.

Porter B. Williamson

CONTENTS

CHAPTER 1
INTRODUCTION

CHAPTER 2
PRINCIPLES OF COMMAND AND MANAGEMENT

CHAPTER 3
PRINCIPLES FOR GOOD HEALTH

CHAPTER 4
PRINCIPLES OF PRIDE AND CONFIDENCE

CHAPTER 5
PRINCIPLES FOR MAKING DECISIONS

CHAPTER 5 (continued)
PRINCIPLES FOR MAKING DECISIONS

CHAPTER 6
PRINCIPLES FOR SUCCESS

CHAPTER 7
PRINCIPLES FOR LIFE AND DEATH